THE INNER JOURNEY:

A GUIDE TO AWAKENING

By Mark Stark

Dedicated to Jen, the love of my life.

Thank you to Trung Nguyen for some editing work.

The doorway is always open.

But who chooses to go through?

Introduction

We're all on the same journey. But only a few really know what that is.

And that's okay. In time we all come to the realization that all along we've been on a long road to reawakening. And when this happens, we can at least see the direction we want to go in and walk in that direction.

As your awareness expands, your life will change dramatically. Reality becomes a much more fluid and flexible creation. One becomes aware of one's role in the creation of it and the active nature of perception and choice. Things begin to manifest more rapidly and with more ease (when it's allowed). As you understand your ability to create you will know that there are no victims in the world, no coincidences, no randomness (only the appearance of such).

Most importantly you will come to know and truly appreciate that the illusion of this world has no power over you (and this is the main message I wish to communicate with the world). Think about that idea for a moment and what the implications are.

It's basically a reversal in thinking from what we are taught to believe about the world and ourselves. From birth a mindset and perspective is taught and ingrained into each of us that we are only these physical bodies moving about on this planet, and the best we can do is stay safe from harm, thrive in the limited way we can, and then die hopefully at age 80 or 90 if we are lucky enough to live that long.

We are taught that we are separate from everything around us. We are taught that we are victims and subject to the power of others.   But as awareness expands the realization sets in that it's possible to choose to set aside the influence of your perceptions for whatever you choose to choose. And that you are not a victim or subject to anyone or anything.

Realize that you are much more than who you think you are.

Imagine for a moment that you are walking in the park enjoying the light of day and trees and sounds of nature. And a man comes up to you and puts a gun into your ribs. What is your reaction?

Our first reaction will be one of 'Oh shit!'. In this situation are you a victim of something outside of yourself? Are you subject to this man's control?   It was considered to be a safe park and after all you were just minding your business and this man approaches asking for your money at gunpoint. I'm not suggesting to see the man and the gun and the circumstance created as not existing, for it exists and if he pulls the trigger your life as you know it may come to an end.

And this is an extreme example but what I am saying is that it is possible to see this and any circumstance in a different light from the way we are normally taught to view it.   You made the choice to walk in the park at this time on this day. A series of choices led up to this moment.   You chose to be here.   The energy you were vibrating created this situation. And just because someone is threatening your life does not mean you have to allow yourself to be disempowered in any way.

Is it not possible to see this man and his energy and allow it to be as you allow your existence to happen?   Is it not possible to see the interconnection of yourself with this man and the oneness of energy that is the two of you, the energy of what is happening in this moment?   That doesn't change the fact that this man is dangerous. But many choices are possible here.   You can react and pee your pants.   Or you can respond and choose to see this situation and this man and yourself in any way you choose. Even with compassion and love.

Now, this does not mean you agree with his choice. Or exclude from potentiality that you kill the attacker even. But when you set aside fear or the desire to control a situation, you allow it to open up and infuse the energy of yourself into what is happening.   And then aren't limitless options and choices allowed and supported in that moment? Let's say for the sake of argument you allow your full energy of being to manifest itself such that you encompass this man with a gun with your energy so that there is no perceived separation between the two of you.   At that point what happens?   At that point fear is set aside and energy is allowed to move and flow.   Suddenly what became a dangerous situation is alleviated into a de-escalation.   The man relaxes his own energy to the point where he does not view the desire to use force.   Pulling the trigger is no longer a likely scenario.

So, words are exchanged and the moment is allowed to resolve itself without violence. When there is no resistance what can be resisted against? This does not mean that you should turn the other cheek.   This does not mean that you should willingly play the role of victim.   There is always room in existence for what you choose.   The idea is to allow your choice to manifest in your life.

So yes, your life is an illusion.   Be aware of what choices you are making on a daily and moment by moment basis and then choose what you wish your life to be. Choose to see yourself from a larger perspective.   Choose to move into your knowing and observe the larger part of what you are. Existence is large enough, allow yourself to reflect soul-essence into your reality, if that is your desire.

Allow the stream and trickle that is your life to broaden and deepen, to become a river. The river of life. Reality is the river we perceive that is life; it is the flow and movement of existence in which choice is created.

Yes, the world and your life are illusion, create it to be as you wish. Knowing the illusion is not real and has no power over you.

As the subtitle states, this book is a guide. As even though we are ultimately all on the same journey, that journey is about empowerment of the self and the knowing of what the true self is and what it means to live from that place. And to get there the most we can hope for or even want is a map with some rough drawings and lines.

You will notice a handful of ideas that tend to re-emerge throughout this book. Repetition is not a bad thing here. Consistency is key as the ideas sink into the layers of your mind and become part of your understanding. Allow your energy to relax.

This book is mainly a gathering of posts from my website over the last five years, a sampling of the more essential thoughts and reflections brought together and presented in a simple and clear way. Websites come and go but books can live forever.

Jen and I just got back from Negril and the countryside in Jamaica. Life is much different there than in Canada. Perhaps one day we will live there. As a minor note, the roads there twist and can be dangerous and are narrow and full of potholes. But they eventually get you to where you want to go. Life is full of bumps but there is pleasure in the experience of it all and a joy that permeates everything.

My best to you all. In respect and appreciation,

Mark

May 20, 2019
Edmonton, Canada

This Journey We Call Life

You can travel all your life as far as your legs or imagination will take you. Around the globe or to the other side of the universe.

Into and out of every kind of relationship or experience.

Conversely, you can study the particles that make up matter and move deep inside particles within particles and the infinite space within space.

Either way, where does it take you?

It takes you to you.

The universe is within (and without) and it is only our own judgments of time and space and everything that creates the distance and separation we perceive.

Move into the space of the smallest particle and you will find that the universe is there.

And you will be at the beginning of where it all begins.

Time and space are your creation and you are here this moment.

And what is your choice?

Your True Nature

"The clearest way into the universe is through a forest wilderness."

-John Muir

Don't be afraid to travel into the untamed wilderness that is your true nature.

That part of you that will never be controlled. That country you have yet to explore.

The summation of all your experiences and movement and growth in this moment in time you call your lifetimes has been a journey of what…?

It has been a journey of remembrance and a coming home, hasn't it?

Fill this life and a million more with every distraction you can imagine, invent or create but are you willing to deny the essence you are?

There is a Well Within You

Quiet your body and mind.

Deliberately.

Move beyond all the activity

and let go of what you think you need to do.

Come to a place of stillness.

This is a place that is not a place.

It is not a beingness.

It is beyond conceptualization.

And it is not a beginning or end.

Don't puzzle about it, just open to it.

Your Greatest Treasure

The sky can fall.

The world can fall apart.

Everything you have known to be your life can turn to ruin.

But there is something that you will never lose.

It's a treasure worth more than all the gold and money and Bitcoin there is.

Your greatest treasure is that which you are. Your essence.

It's your real worth. Beyond measure or compare.

It represents an ease and vitality that cannot be sold or stolen or given away.

The essence you are

is the treasure in this turbulent and unpredictable world.

Do you choose to accept this?

Do you choose to reflect this?

Do you choose to live this?

Your Sense of Essence

Connecting with your essence is about choosing and living more from who you are.

In a world with infinite distraction it's important to be aware of the mind's pull into contraction and distraction.

Living consciously is about embracing the simplicity of who you are at the core.

It's an awareness of who you are and living from that place.

Not the other way around where you live like a leaf blowing in the wind from one situation or occurrence to the next.

How can anyone be empowered if they are reacting to anything 'external'?

Do what you need to do to connect with your essence. Be aware.

And you will get a feeling sense of that deeper energy.

Cultivate that feeling and see how it interconnects with everything.

Call it a sense of essence.

Explore it and connect deeper.

The Gift of Pause

It doesn't take the study of Upanishads or sutras up on some cliff in Nepal.

It doesn't take years of chanting Om or genuflecting before a Guru or backpacking across the world.

You don't need crystals or spirit guides or Jesus or Jehovah.

You don't need any knowledge of spiritual terminology or practices.

You don't need a kinesiology muscle or consciousness calibration test.

There are no steps or techniques.

It doesn't cost money and doesn't require much at all (just a bit of willingness and openness).

It is simplicity itself. (Which is why so few are drawn to it)

In fact, pausing is about doing nothing at all. The art of letting go.

Connecting deeper and deeper. Feeling what arises but letting go to the point where it is just you with... yourself.

And in a moment, you will meet that deeper place of You.

And nothing will be the same.

In a moment of pause, find out what is possible.

Chasing After the World

Perhaps the biggest dis-ease in the world today is living life on the Hamster Wheel.

The constant grind and struggle and pursuit of something: Money. Job. Career. Relationships. Success. Balance. Health. Beauty. Approval. Enlightenment. Peace. Whatever.

It becomes a type of internal prison and often people aren't even aware of how insidious and pervasive it affects their whole life.

> *That which you chase, you will never have.*
>
> *All the chase leads to is more of the chase.*
>
> (And if that is what you want. Go for it.)

I've talked about it before: don't try.

Just choose. Choose you.

They don't teach this in schools. There is no Harvard MBA for this. In fact, society teaches quite the opposite, don't they?

I like this Zen gatha:

> *'Chasing after the world*
>
> *brings only chaos.*
>
> *Allowing it all to come to me*
>
> *Brings peace.'*

We are here to explore and create and desire is not a bad thing. But a distinction needs to be made:

It's the choice not to give your power away to the world but to be you.

Nothing Lacking

I grew up with a certain awareness of existence. But there was always the feeling or experience that something was lacking in myself.

The boy became a teenager who became an adult and still the feeling of something not quite right often seemed to be there. Buried.

And it wasn't until I became radically honest with myself that I could see and acknowledge that I was exploring life from a perspective of insufficiency. And basically everyone does the same thing – if they are being honest. As the reality we exist in is based on the perception of separation (which is created through judgment).

And one day I chose to explore existence from a place of sufficiency. And sufficiency goes far, far beyond self-esteem. It goes to the core of what existence is. Alignment and harmony with the universe and your interconnection and unity with everything.

You will never truly know yourself

until you recognize your equality and relationship

with everything.

There is No End to It All

It's spiritual fallacy that at some point in your existence you will stop being here.

That you will stop reincarnating.

(Why do you think you chose to be here now?)

When you awaken,

guess what?

Life carries on.

The journey never ends.

And would you want it any other way?

And all of this doesn't mean you will not be exploring other ways of living and existing.

It doesn't mean that you are limited in any way.

The Importance of Trusting Yourself

Intuition will tell you that you can trust yourself more. And that the answers you seek are within.

This speaks to the sufficiency of who we are within existence.

No one is greater or lesser than you.

Yet how often do you give your power away to anything and everything outside of yourself? (just think about money and sex, for starters)

If there is nothing greater than you, why are you in a habit of deferring to others on your journey to discover the greater part of who you are?

Why do you defer to others for guidance when the whole point of the exploration is to become intimate with yourself?

Trust yourself. Know yourself.

And at that point everything will fall into place. You will have the answers you seek (and come to value the questions as more vital).

And you will know the mysteries of the universe as very few do.

An Effective Way to Meditate and Grow

There are many ways to meditate.

And there an equal number of ways to waste your time and not get anywhere.

Why is this? For different reasons but mainly because meditation too often becomes just another 'doing'. Not a 'being', which is the whole purpose.

Remember that meditation is a way to say 'No!' to the spinning of your mind; it's a way to say 'No!' to the giving your power of away to the illusion that is the world. But ultimately, it's about opening yourself to a deeper understanding of things. An awareness.

And it only takes a moment and you can do it anywhere, anytime.

(Forget the religions and the gurus and any source outside of yourself.)

Method? Okay:

Allow your energy to encompass everything in existence.

The Consciousness of Humanity

Humanity has achieved technological advancement

but has it achieved anything else?

Not really.

View the movement of humanity

over the centuries and millennia

and you will see that the consciousness of humanity

has not grown.

So where do we go from here?

A healthy first step would be to set aside our arrogance

and look at the world, ourselves and each other

with that sense of wonder and play

that we had as children.

With those eyes.

And then to ask ourselves, what is possible.

On Enlightenment and Perception

From an online forum in 2009:

'I recall a conversation with a friend who had a problem with the seeming duality of violence and love in the world, and the endless parade of "victims" in the world. He cited an example of an old lady who was killed. Within this context he asked how does one become enlightened and I replied (using the extreme example) that until you see that you are both the victim and the murderer, and the very knife that kills, there is no enlightenment. As long as something or someone is outside of self there is fear, and with fear, endless defining and separation and no ownership or remembrance of our immortal, stainless Nature. Being limitless means encompassing all things. As you both observed, 'this-and-that', not 'this-or-that'.

Most people realize that they are more than their mere body or mind. We create our own realities through perception. But if we are the beauty of the dove that sweeps low across a pale blue sky; the laughter and happiness of a child in the sandbox; the glance and subsequent caresses of two lovers meeting after months apart, then we also inhabit that which spawns war and calamity and ignorance. Not separate from it. But with true knowledge comes the ability to live the knowledge. To move through it and be.

Eventually all concepts (incl. personality, 'choice', etc.) and definitions collapse under their own form or weight. The prism becomes the mirror and the mirror dissolves. 'Brahman' creates and consumes illusion. It is no wonder that some Zen monks and Hindu sages do not speak, do little and just smile or laugh.'

Within Us All

Look beyond the surface of appearances and you will see it.

It is something which is in every person.

The richest and poorest. The young and old.

It is the energy of choice.

And it is this energy that creates our world and lives.

It is this energy which speaks to the equality and sufficiency and brilliance of the one and the whole.

Observe it and you will see it in yourself.

Playing with Perception

"The strange fragments of reality make patterns in your head sometimes. They form a collage that is static for a few moments, giving you the feeling that you are on the edge of perception that might make all the rest of it a little more meaningful... Very probably all perceptions are second hand."

> -**Darker Than Amber** (1966), John D. MacDonald

I love reading John D. MacDonald novels. Besides knowing how to tell a first-rate story he is an intelligent, articulate, thoughtful and perceptive author who had no problem giving pause in the narrative to share his/Travis McGee's thoughts on the world, people and life.

Relating to his quote, what happens when you open the doors of perception and open yourself beyond a limited, narrow perspective of existence?

Your perspective of what reality is will change. It will not be a lineality of time or space or based on an adherence to 'cause and effect'. The word 'fragments' as John D. used and described is applicable as the supporting structure of how the mind glues everything into one neat conception of things becomes loose and you will observe a restructuring of that structure into something more flexible and expansive and encompassing that will more accurately fit a larger conception of what existence is.

Perception is related to choice. And our perception of things determines our experience. And the collapse of the old way of seeing the world will be replaced by awareness and an awareness of what does hold everything together.

And it will be a radical departure from how the universe is currently seen.

The Pleasures of the Simple Life

"I turned my head and saw, beyond the shoulder of my beloved, the empty copper sea, hushed and waiting, as if the world had paused between breaths."
–Empty Copper Sea (1978), John D. MacDonald

It is worth asking yourself:

How can I bring more ease into my life?

Without creating conscious moments of pause, reflection and relaxation of what quality will your life have?

Deep slow breathing. Relaxation. Let go of the tensions and stresses of the world and open up your inner sight and feeling.

Sip on some tea and reread some books you love or find an author that nourishes you.

Find new ways to free up time in your life and explore new things.

It is the simple pleasures that make a life worth living.

Does this go without saying?

Death Before Dying

You will always be in survival/fear mode until you shift your perspective to view the world from a radically different way:

From your deepest inner self.

Your essence.

Why is this so? As only from that perspective a new freedom opens up based on the understanding that

there is no death

only creation and your experience of it.

Until we bring ease and clarity into our lives, *living in the world is the hard part.* Physical dying is easy as then we are at Home in peace (again). And the process of life never really ends.

Recognize this and live from your essence and the 'Sword of Damocles' that hangs over your life will cease to be a factor in your choices. You will be one of the few who are truly free.

Imagine what your life would be if you lived from this new perspective.

Will you give yourself this freedom?

Two Things to Remember

One:

Your conscious mind has a very limited perspective of things.

Thus, the importance of letting go

and trusting the 'more' that is you.

Two:

To the degree that you see yourself as separate from the world and God/Goddess/The All-That-Is, that will be your reality and existence.

Observe that separation (that you have chosen) and this awareness will allow you to choose more.

Makes sense, right?

Opening the Doors of Perception

"Who in the world am I? Ah, that's the great puzzle."
–Alice in Wonderland

When you relax your definitions of reality and who and what you think you are it becomes possible to engage the world in a more fluid and open way. You can actually choose how you want to see yourself and the world.

For instance: by default, your mind will see separation in everything. It will see that relationship between yourself and everything and everyone. But it is possible to shift your perspectives and perception to one of something else. To see the oneness or essence. But it must be your choice and actively chosen so that the mind is guided in that direction.

Or, you can choose to see yourself as whatever you choose and explore that in your life. You can literally go in any direction. You can engage active perception and actively create your reality with your conscious mind instead of being a passive participant.

To know yourself is to realize that ultimately you are energy and choice. There are many posts on the website that talk about and relate to this for those of you who want to explore in that direction.

Never forget, this world is fiction. Your life is a story. Nothing is real. What would you like your narrative to be?

<Cheshire Cat wink >

Shifting your Perception of the World

Your perception of the world, of existence, is not a static thing.

Think about how powerful that is.

Think of the opportunity that is and the unlimited possibilities.

You are not separate from anyone else.

You are not separate from anything.

The tension and heartache that comes from living in this world only happens because we have bought into something that is not true.

Open yourself to the possibility of more.

See beyond what your mind perceives as "real" to a place where your heart knows the truth of something much larger.

It has nothing, absolutely nothing to do with religion or sidestepping into another box in which to view the world.

It's about connecting with the essence of energy that you are. An essence that ultimately unites everything.

In the space between your thoughts and perceptions and moments you call your life....

you will begin to get a sense of it.

If you are ready, interested, and choose to explore that direction.

Say "Yes!" and Let it Begin~

What are you exploring in your life?

What would you like to explore?

There is a road you will be traveling down.

(In this lifetime or not.)

And the road is hidden from view.

To see it you have to move in a direction you have never tried before.

You have to look in the mirror and see that you are the journey.

You are the expression.

You are existence.

If you feel these words resonate in any way within you, do something about it.

Be transformed.

Set your life on fire.

Say "Yes" and let it all begin.

(Do you think there is any end to this journey we are on?)

Bring These Ideas into Your Life

There is nothing in this world you have to react to

When you live from your center, things get pretty simple.

As you see things as they are.

And ultimately nothing can pull you from your place of being – unless you allow it.

Notice I didn't say that you can ignore what happens around you.

You do need to make choices. But it's helpful to realize and remember that

You are the energy of choice

This will give you a flexibility to go with the flow

and a foundation of understanding that will carry you through

when the universe occasionally knocks you off your feet.

If you are not willing to observe your illusions in life, there will come a time when you will be forced to.

(perhaps not in this lifetime but there will be a time in your existence)

Awareness Just is

When you make the choice to expand your existence it becomes clear after a certain point that "your" awareness isn't yours.

Awareness just is.

It is a constancy and encompasses everything. Beyond the mind's perspective.

As you engage this awareness your life will change as the movement has already been made to 'open up':

You will know things about yourself and others intuitively.

You will know when someone is lying (to you or themself).

You will readily be able to observe energy blocks in yourself and others.

You will recognize that little voice inside that nudges you 'left' when the 'right' you have chosen a thousand times before leads to a result you did not want (like getting clipped by a car and dying.)

You will observe brilliance in everyone and everything and see the essence you share.

Increasingly you will sense or know things before they happen.

You will observe the relationship between empowerment and choice.

You will see the impact of your choices.

You will know that your life can be as fluid as a river and responsive if you allow it.

You will see that 'cause and effect' is just an illusion, like everything else.

You will observe the futility and limitation imposed by your mind's insistence on judgment (and how it will still be a part of your life up to a point).

You will know that oneness and love are not just ideas.

You will come to know that there are truly no limits to your existence (but those you choose on some level).

You will see that the brilliance you are shines brighter than all the suns in the universe.

~ ~ ~

(Do what you want with your life but the world has enough zombies in it.

Last count was over 7 billion.)

Shifting into the Energy Perspective

When people begin their journey into exploring concepts that will expand and redefine their lives, it is a process where the mind will be involved.   The mind — your mind, not something outside of you — will see these things from the outside looking in.

It is a bit like window shopping.   Looking at new ideas from the outside through the glass.   Through the filters and perspectives of the mind, rather than from your true self. Analyzing and justifying the possibility of new choices, not choosing and living from the new place. Observe how the mind will control and limit and reduce things until it is guided to a new realization of things.

And the difference is not trivial.   It is like the difference between looking at postcard of the ocean and swimming naked in the ocean. It is the difference between the mind's conceptualization and a living, breathing knowing within.

Feel the difference between these two statements:

I am stuck in my routine of life but there are possibilities in the universe.

or

I am the energy of possibility.

Another example. Observe the shift in perspective:

Am I part of the energy of everything?

or

I am energy.

My journey has been one of shifting into and consciously choosing this new way of living. It is an empowerment that is based in awareness and commanding of the mind. Consciously giving it a direction.

This shift into new ways of seeing is and will be a dramatic shift in your life as you choose it. And it will apply to everything as our beingness encompasses everything.

A practical use of this awareness is creating and designing your life in ways you choose.

I want a loving, sexy partner/I do not have a loving sexy partner.

or

I am a loving, sexy person/partner.

Notice the difference in energy and perspective. The first is one of seeking and implies a need. A perspective of lack. Like the universe designed you with something missing. The second statement is one of awareness, joy and energy, reflecting and creating.

Feel the energy of what you want and the direction you choose. *Know your choice and own it.* The energy you are is what creates so live from this place.

Sometimes I am able to create what I want.

or

I am creative energy.

What is your awareness of yourself? The mind will define and control your existence at every step but just keep directing it. See it as the tool it is.   Have fun with this idea and start consciously designing your life and movements.

The ideas you are exploring will mature into a deep knowing and understanding. Eventually the choices you make will start coming from the self.   Your true essence. More and more anyway.

And does the journey ever end?

Observation and the Art of Allowance

It is interesting and a great learning experience to observe just how much struggle we create in our daily lives and how much energy we expend on things that are not working. Or towards things that are not what we want in our life.

An example would be working at a job you don't really like. It is not the work itself that usually requires much energy but our approach to it. The thoughts we have towards it and the resistance we create and 'allow'.

Observe all of your choices in life. And if you want to, move in the direction of clarity and simplicity. Breathe and feel your natural energy and allow your choices to be. To happen.

It is our thinking that creates the weight and density in our lives. Actively guide your mind in a new direction when you observe it going in a direction not of your choosing.

Remind yourself as often as necessary that you are not here to be stressed or to feel disempowered. You are not here to grind out a living and to reach a "someday".

Explore possibility and probability and choose to lighten your life. Everything can become simple and the exploration changes to one of an expression of the ease of your energy.

This is the art of allowance.

The Practice of Intention

There is an idea in yoga of 'sankalpa' which is basically setting an intention before the session. A resolution. A similar thing would be planting an idea into your subconscious mind as you drift off to sleep.

Intention only works with any real impact if we carry it into our daily lives. Choosing as we live in each moment.

Think of intention as the setting of a direction we give our minds as a guide or reference for what we want to explore or create.

Keep the intention simple and positive and clear. Feel it. Feel how it is part of who you are already. For in truth it is. The energy you are encompasses everything else in existence.

This Moment Called Now

Anticipation of the future creates tension in your body and mind.

It pulls us from being present and seeing what is happening and dilutes the quality and intensity of life.

We can use our imagination to inform and create our reality and lives – it's what we do any way, isn't it? But why not just let this moment be enough?

This moment in which you are in is enough.

It is sufficient. You are sufficient.

There is no great need that needs filling immediately this very moment.

The future will take care of itself - if you take care of yourself right now.

Trust in your ability and power to choose in the moment as events arise and unfold.

Trust in your ability to allow things to come into your life and practice acceptance.

Trust in your ability to go in any direction you choose.

Trust in your ability to respond effectively rather than react to things in this world.

As there is no 'greater' source or power than what lies deep within you.

You were not created as a lesser being and there is no lesser being in all of existence.

A homeless person, a president of a country or a billionaire are no better or worse than each other. They are each simply choosing and experiencing life in their own way. Nothing is inherently greater or lesser than another. Observe that. (Religion would say otherwise but that is another topic.)

Recognize what is being said here and how it applies to your life.

Just because something is not manifested in this very moment before your eyes doesn't mean a lick. Stop playing games thinking the universe has to be a certain way.

The Problem with Goal-setting

Life is a journey. It is a great joy and opportunity to explore in any direction and to choose our empowerment. Simply being in the moment, connected with yourself, your beingness and essence, you can create or move in any direction and enjoy the unfolding. You are sufficient.

The goal-setting approach affirms and creates a distance or obstacle where there does not need to be one. Goal-setting does not facilitate the awareness that that which you seek is part of you already.

Instead of goal-setting simply observe the movement of energy of that which you are. Observe your life as it is happening. Observe what your choices are creating and make choices that will move you to where you would like to be in your life. And allow that. For within you this very moment is everything you can possibly desire or create. There is no need to struggle or go through hoops.

We have lost touch with our innate ability to simply allow manifestation. What do you think Jesus was doing when he turned water into wine? Do you doubt that this ability and more exists within you as well?

It is worthwhile to observe that many of the things people want and their methodologies and striving to achieve them is just a reflection of their own perspectives of not being 'good-enough' or lack.

We fear not being able to bring into our lives that which we want so we play games and roles that remove us from our beingness. And we love the contraction as that affirms our beliefs and conception of existence and at that point we can just throw our hands up in the air and say "See? That's how it is. Why bother trying?"

But being conscious is about being aware of our choices and choosing. And taking that ownership of your life is a task few want to have.

Create whatever you wish in your life. Manifest yourself in any way you choose. But why not do so from a place of empowerment?

Save the World? Start with Yourself

The world we see is a reflection of what is inside of us. It is a reflection of our perceptions, beliefs, choices and movement. It is a reflection of our awareness.

Earth at this time is an interesting place to be exploring and living and creating. There are many inherent challenges and possibilities and often our greatest opportunities are disguised as roadblocks or as our struggles. Observe the flow and movement of your life. What issues bring you stress or conflict? What problems are you dealing with or what issues are you struggling with to resolve? What are changes that you would like to see in the world?

A lot of people try to create change in the world or in their own lives but do so without going within and truly realizing that creation comes from within ourselves. We are not separate from that spring of creative energy that gives rise to everything, *we are the very essence of it.*

Instead of being overly concerned with the physical manifestation of what is happening in our lives, the ups and downs or the outward appearance, it is important to look at what is happening inside of ourselves as we go about living our lives. How are you reacting to what is happening around you at any one given moment? What is your energy? Notice your thoughts and thought process, fears, body tension, the inner psychologies and games at play, etc. and where and what you are giving your power to.

In times of war or conflict for example people make judgments as automatic reactions and there is a strong rush to take sides. There is often a this-person versus that-person or one group or country versus another. This type of demarcation actually solidifies the conflict into more concrete terms and perpetuates things, often spiraling conflict into very destructive outcomes. Groups that form an "anti-" this or that such as anti-war, anti-abortion, or anti-anything are actually giving their power away. They are giving their energy to perpetuating the very problems they are trying to get rid of. Being anti-war is not a state that allows resolution of conflict. Pro-peace is better but even that is giving energy to a side in the conflict, as "peace" is the opposite of war, two sides of the same coin really.

In creation there is no denying anything. Everything is manifest. There is only energy and what your choice is in the moment. What you allow to manifest in your life. And pushing against anything is only playing a game of denial with yourself and maintaining what you are pushing against.

Acknowledge what is happening around you but look past and through what is happening. See the bigger perspective and observe how reality is not a static creation. To move through a wall that is blocking you in your life, simply stop trying to push it down. See it, appreciate it for what it is and what it reflects — say a limit of perception — and soften your energy around it, relax your energy and allow another direction in your life. Choose something else. It is best to focus on what we truly want, let's say in this example of an alternative to ant-war or pro-peace, lending our energy to living in harmony and well-being. And this starts with ourselves.

So instead of trying to resolve problems by approaching it at the level of the problem, try taking a step back and breathing and maybe even some meditation or some type of new perspective. Play some music and dance and smile and laugh and play and have some happy-crazy fun. Whatever opens your energy. For when you raise your consciousness it affects the world around you and the way you see the world. Perception changes. And what was once a problem or issue may cease to even be an issue at all in your life if you come from your beingness. For in your beingness there is no lack or struggle or effort. Energy flows and we can allow your lives to reflect this awareness. We can allow our lives to become an amazing organic living reflection of the beautiful energy essence we are.

This isn't wishful Hippie ideas but actually how reality works. And do you want to but your head against the universe or create flow with it?

By all means take action and live boldly! Live large! But do so from a place of empowerment. Do so from your beingness and energy, not from your mind's reaction. Save the world by saving yourself first and you will find that you have done more than you realize. For the exploration and expansion of consciousness is a not a little thing. It is everything.

There is nothing separating you from anything else in existence. The door in front of you is open. It is up to you to step forward and move through it.

The world doesn't need a savior. But it does need you.

The Love that is

You will move through your existence in the way you will until a point is reached where you will no longer deny yourself of the love you have for yourself and all existence. For in truth, the love that you are is the love of all things, and the love of all things is the love you are.

This is the empowerment you are moving toward, the realization, the movement. All of your experiences and exploration in all of your lifetimes are leading you to an opening which will be the expansion of consciousness and awareness.

And no stone or pebble will be left untouched or unturned.

Letting Go

Feel the truth of this statement:

The only limitations you have in life are the ones you settle for.

The limitations created by the choices you make to perceive yourself and life a certain way, and then you say to yourself "this is how it is". And isn't this the way humans live? From green young saplings at birth to stiff brown branches within the span of not so many years. The hardening of the heart and perception in different ways.

Remember times as a child when all you wanted to do was explore and play and have fun? Adults would tell you one thing and your first reaction to them would be "But that's silly!", an intuition and knowing from within. Over time people stop questioning things. They stop asking why. They stop taking that leap of faith into unknown territory, the uncharted landscape of our inner world (and outer universe). We stop questioning what the mind perceives as fact or something that is obvious so why bother.

It is our nature to question and grow and experience all that life is. Yet how easy it is to settle into "comfortable" lives until that irritant arrives. Perhaps it is a nagging dissatisfaction from within that something is not the way you truly want. Something feels off or not in alignment in your life. Perhaps everything. Or perhaps you get hit by a Mack truck in the way the universe can deliver when we are not listening: disease or illness or death or tragedy happens. And our life is up-ended completely.

Observe your life carefully... set the judgments aside and just simply see where your choices have led you... be honest and see the influence that your judgments and fears have had on your life. And the fear of fear. Observe how perhaps at one point you gave up your red wagon and sand shovel and settled for an adding machine and ledger. You stopped playing and being child-like. Observe the level of control you have exerted in your life... the trying, the stress and effort and contraction. Breathe in deeply and relax.

How many try to control their lives or use some idea of 'change' as a substitution for a real exploration and the movement into their beingness? Oftentimes people take up a new pursuit or sport, a new relationship or job, take a vacation or they change their wardrobe, or even shift into a slightly new way of thinking about themselves. But is this growth or just change? Have they let go of anything really or are they still operating from within the same paradigm that they are trying to shift out of? How satisfying is it living like that?

When was the last time you took a truly deep breath and felt that sense of "Ahhhh. This is good!"

Observe closely the influence of your mind in your life and you will see the extent to which the mind interferes, limits, reduces and tries to control things as a way of 'surviving' and ensuring its continuity when it is not consciously directed. The result is quite crippling. And so through lifetimes there is only very small movement and shifts into awareness. Very little growth if any.

And from one perspective that is okay but is it your choice? Is it what you really desire and want right now? The energy you are is one of love. It is one that opens and encompasses all things. It is a brilliance beyond compare. Take a moment to feel the truth of this statement and bring it into your life...

Now, explore this beautiful idea: releasing control of your life and living from the awareness you have of your deeper self. Your energy and beingness. Let go of control and embrace the mystery and vastness of life…. of your own beingness.

Your mind is always trying to solve the great puzzle of who you are. It attempts to define and measure and scrambles for answers and then spends so much time and energy justifying choices. This is what we do. But our beingness is undefinable. How liberating and freeing would it be to simply acknowledge that you cannot control your life and that you do not have the answers to the puzzling? The illusion of control can be created but is that truly living or is it simply playing a game with yourself?

When you explore your fears and the incessant striving and trying of your existence, there is movement into a deeper understanding. The realization that you lack nothing. The space opens up for a more genuine and real exploration into new choices. Into growth and empowerment.

Before you achieve the beingness that you seek, a letting go takes place. This is what you are here to explore and discover and take part in. To enjoy. You have a choice to make: to live your life from the shore or to jump in the water. To go play in the ocean.

Rediscover your ability and talent to play and wonder and explore and love. Life is a treasure so go out and get wet.

Why We are Here

We are here to experience it all. The experience of existence. From the larger perspective there is no good or bad or judgment, just the experience of existence. *Your soul-essence expands and grows through your choices and experience.*

The larger part of you craves life and is life energy. Breathe and allow your energy to flow and create how you will.

Fear is What We Make it to be

Most people have some type of fear of dying. It is not their greatest fear but it exists. But how real is this fear? How real is fear?

When you move into the awareness of yourself as energy, you will connect with an energy that has a constancy to it. A continuity. An energy of *constancy and continuity* that extends far beyond what is perceived to be your single lifetime.

If you slip off the curb one morning and a car hits you and you die, you know that it will not be the end of you. Yes, your ego-personality, that framework people usually live by will re-integrate with soul-essence but life will carry on. Your energy will simply extend itself into another creation. Another experience. Another lifetime. Life can never be extinguished.

Explore this idea if you want and see what an illusion fear really is.

Connect with your energy and feel this to be true. Explore your interconnection with everything around you and all of existence.

Open to it All

Love is everything. It opens up everything.

When the choice is made to go within and to start appreciating the self and all, make it a practical application and bring it into your daily life. It is not a thought game but a choice to truly live and be alive.

Choose it in every moment.

And watch your life and awareness grow beyond anything you can imagine.

The Universe in a Grain of Sand

Have you ever seen one of those fractal videos where no matter how much you move into it, it never ends?

Go within.

Just as the smallest particle extends itself outward to encompass everything, the love you have for yourself extends to all that is.

That which you are is without beginning or end.

So be vulnerable.

The further you go within, the deeper your outward exploration into time, consciousness and the universe.

Wealth

If you see yourself as separate from anything around you, then you will never find the wealth and abundance that you desire and seek.

For there is not enough money or gold in the world to fill that hole, that perception, as it is one that will fuel your perspectives of lack and insufficiency in your existence.

Energy

Energy is everything that is. Everything.

That includes what we see, touch, smell, hear, and feel and everything else. It is the trees, people, buildings and everything in our environment. All that we perceive is a perception or interpretation of energy. It is the trees, people, buildings and objects of our environment. A thought is energy. Desire is energy. A perspective of time is energy. Ideas of past and future or relationships is a judgment of energy.

Granted yes, it is all energy judged and reduced through the filters of our minds but it is still energy.

And all energy has consciousness, is consciousness.   If the particles of a wall were vibrating at a different rate you would perceive it as something else, water perhaps, and be able to put your hand through it or walk through.

You can call this energy whatever you want as it will be judged. Some call it Chi, Qi, Prana, atomic, electromagnetic, etc. Love energy or simply love.

What does this mean to you? What would you like it to mean?

Once we move into the awareness that the universe is energy then it becomes easier to see and to truly know and appreciate that we ourselves are energy. We are the creative energy essence of existence and can mold or shape energy into any form we choose. We can shape and create our life to be what it will.

We can manifest our talents and abilities in their fullness and more. We can create and choose in any direction and follow the flow of this energy into any new direction at any point. We can re-frame or explore perspectives and beliefs or any concept. We can explore our sufficiency and true wealth within existence, as existence. We can live from a timeless, limitless perspective and more, not contraction or reduction. We can move beyond 3rd dimensional reality into the inter-dimensionality of existence.

Energy is all things and the universe will allow everything.

Now this does not mean you will walk out the door and command the sky to clear and become sunny or to form money out of thin air. But engaging your sense of awareness and seeing everything as energy does open you to the possibility of it. It will open you more to what is around you, how the energy is flowing and what is ripe for you to allow into your life, easily and effortlessly.

It will open you to new choices and probabilities which will lead you in the direction of other choices. It will open you to a limitless perspective of existence and your connection with everything.

These are just possibilities when we get in touch with our true nature. There are no limits once we expand our awareness and begin to play with this as it is a new way of living and being. A new way of seeing. It is a new paradigm. It is the empowerment of you.

Imagine yourself unfettered and unshackled, truly empowered and in command of your existence. Move with the energy of who you are and start making choices that reflect this deeper knowing of who you are. What would you most like to explore and create in your life?

Listen to the audio recording I produced called **The Limitless Self**.

Always and Forever

As we live this human experience let's recognize that we're here to empower ourselves.

There are a million ways to reduce and contract our existence.

But we can choose to be in this world and ~*whatever circumstances arise*~ we can choose to move through it by being connected to our source.

It's about more than faith.

It's about knowing who you are and knowing that in each moment we have a choice.

It's about knowing that we are, in fact, the energy of choice.

Connecting with your Sense of Awareness

Meditation is not a doing. It is a being. A connecting with your sense of awareness.

Observe the difference.

This applies to any spiritual practice you may have, like yoga, energy work, etc. but can also extend into every moment of your life… if you go in that direction and choose it.

Live in awareness in all that you do.

The form and forms of our lives are simply the physical manifestation.

Love is not a doing either, although it can manifest as that. Love is an energy of allowance that allows our choices. So ultimately, we choose from the energy and love that we are and creation is us. We are not separate from the world around us but infuse it with our energy.

It is important to see beyond the form of things.

The Puzzle Called Enlightenment

Enlightenment is simply about connecting with your deeper sense of awareness. Clearly seeing things as they are. In a practical sense, seeing through the illusion of the world.

But enlightenment is also a game for the mind. A puzzle and fuel for the mind. Which is okay. Give it some candy and make it happy.

But the question arises: how do you connect with your sense of awareness? It is a place very few really connect with as it is far beyond the five physical senses.

The simplest answer I can share is that you do it by choosing it.

By going in that direction and exploring deeper and living the choice. How big is your desire to understand the bigger picture and to experience something more in your life? Allow yourself to move with that flow of energy.

As a practice, meditation can be a useful and there are, of course, many practices that can facilitate an expansion. As long as at some point you take the hinges off the doors.

It basically comes down to observing yourself and the world — without the filter of judgment, as much as possible.

Observe your choices and choose more.

When you connect with your sense of awareness you are choosing limitlessness.

Aging is Not a Given

Are your choices aging you?

Have you ever wondered if there was another way to live, one where we don't age in the usual way?

This world offers many things to push and pull against. If we let it.

Make relaxation more than a part of your life, make it your way of life. That ease of being. FEEL IT. Practice letting go and allowing your life to be an expression of allowance.

It is the friction and tension and weight of our lives that ages us. Our choices and perspectives. Our choice not to go with the flow of things and move with that deeper river of energy.

Cultivate a daily practice that will replenish your energy and mind. Whatever that may be for you. And open yourself to something more.

The Fountain of Youth Does Exist

Have you ever observed how a salamander, starfish or worm can regrow parts of themselves?

Have you ever paid attention to how many mammals and birds and insects have the capacity to communicate on a non-verbal level, telepathically, beyond what humans allow themselves?

Have you ever observed how some things just flow into your existence without so much as a thought? How manifestation just happens?   Have you ever observed your own body's innate capacity to replicate skin cells and the miracle of how it heals itself when cut or harmed?

Do you honestly believe that the cells of your body were created with any inherent limits? Do you honestly believe that you have any limits?

Scientists only ever discover the limits of their own bias. Their own perceptions. For how can they accept what they are not willing to observe and look at without their filters on?

Over time humans have adopted belief structures that reflect such limits. And they have done so for they fear their brilliance. They fear their beingness.

Your body and cell structures have the capacity for infinite regeneration and rejuvenation.

The Fountain of Youth is within. *It is your awareness of yourself as energy.* You are the master alchemist.

Doubt not what you are capable of, if only gave yourself the chance.

The Order of Things

"The life of man is of no greater importance to the universe than that of an oyster."

-David Hume

You are an integral part of the universe.

A piece of it that is connected with everything.

But that does not mean that you are more important than the donkey chewing on hay.

Or the slug that crawls up the leaf.

Or the prison convict or janitor or politician.

Or anyone or thing.

Eventually you will tire of your ego-personality and move beyond it.

To something more broadening.

Until then enjoy who you are and the role and games you play.

Let's not take ourselves too seriously.

Raise Your Vibration

Before you dismiss this as Hippy-speak, give me a moment.

One of the benefits of energy work/healing in general is that it raises your vibration.

And raising your vibration is about living your fullest expression and enjoying life.

The only thing that keeps us down is the mind's game of fear so it is essential to observe your state of being and choices.

Observe and observe some more just how much fear limits and reduces your life. And then choose the other direction.

Conscious choice must be exercised here. To be aware and then to direct your existence. As fear is so ingrained in our thinking and way of life it is not immediately apparent just how pervasive it is.

When we are open and enjoying life and connected with our beingness then our vibration is naturally high. There are no impediments to choosing and moving and creating in any direction. There is flexibility and joy and ease.

There is also the knowing that no matter what circumstance or situation you find yourself in, you can choose not to play the game of contraction and fear.

Nothing can disempower you if you choose not to allow it.

The Experience of Time

A boy becomes a young man. The young man becomes a middle-aged man. The middle-aged man becomes an old man.

A girl becomes a young woman. The young woman becomes a middle-aged woman. The middle-aged woman becomes an old woman.

There is the passage of time.

We look in the mirror and depending on our age we see a face looking back at us that is commensurate with an age. A face with a body to match.

We tell ourselves "I am now 20 years old." Or "I am now 72 years old." and there is a movement of time, a perception of time and aging, isn't there? And psychologies which are deeply ingrained.

People move through their lives being utterly dominated by time. Not commanding their lives but allowing time to enslave them.

"It is 10pm. I have to work tomorrow. Time for bed. Or I won't get my 7.5 hours of sleep. And if I do not get my 7.5 hours of sleep I will be trashed tomorrow. I have to catch the bus at 6:58am so I can be at work by 7:52am."

Just the idea of 'tomorrow' is removing you from where you are now. Your sufficiency in this moment. Your beingness. Perceptions of past and future, and what are the past and future but concepts based on judgments of the present moment. Judgments which disempower you.

And we do things like create 'bucket lists':

"Before I die, I want to go to Greece and visit the islands."

Or, "When I retire, I will take up photography which I have always thought about but never pursued."

See the relationship between time and choice?

We create our experience of life. Of time.

Go ahead and create your bucket list. *Or live forever*.

And you live forever by stepping out of time. By seeing it as the illusion it is.

Choose your limitlessness and realize that you are possibility and choice. It is inherent in who you are. Inherent in your energy. That does not mean that you have to manifest in any one particular way at a given moment. That would be a game of control, not allowance.

You were once a little boy or girl. You inhaled oxygen into your little lungs and stood open before the universe. Open to magic and possibility. Open to life. Imagination engaged.

And in that moment, you just were. No past, no future.

That same 'moment' as now. And not even that.

The experience of existence. Not time.

Observe your perception of time. The definitions by which you age yourself.

Be open for understanding that there is much more than the limits you have defined your life and choices by up till now.

Nourish Yourself

The greatest gift you can give to yourself is yourself. *The gift of You*. The gift of compassion and love. Most people intuitively know this but few are consciously aware that loving the self can truly expand your existence.

Through the practice of living in awareness and observing everything without judgment we can see just how prevalent and pervasive our judgments are. We judge ourselves more harshly than anyone or anything else can ever judge us and it is a death-like grip that contracts every part of our lives, and with this reduction the choices that are possible in our lives.

Judgments come from the mind which is a tool which must be directed or it will continue on its own path. Most of us live from the mind, not our beingness. So observe your thoughts, feelings, actions, non-actions, observe your choices and everything. Choose to be intimately aware of yourself. Explore your perspectives and beliefs and limitations.

Move into your beingness and allow yourself the choice of not judging your judgments for as human beings we will judge. To live without judgment we would not be in physical form and physicality can be a lot of fun. The trick is to reduce the judgment and soften your grips. Relax your mind so it is not interfering in your life. Use your minds to be conscious and to enhance your existence. They are something to be observed and appreciated, like everything else.

Part of loving the self is releasing control and allowing others their choices. You do not have to agree with anyone's choice but see how trying to control anyone else is a game of disempowerment and an illusion within illusion. Allow others to live how they want and get in touch with what you want in your life and what you want to express to yourself and the world.

When you love yourself – truly, honestly and completely love yourself – your energy relaxes and opens and interacts more freely with everything around you as you will see yourself as part of everything around you. Your essence, the energy you are, is then reflected in the world and universe and moves with everything.

When this happens we feel more alive, connected, healthy and joyful. There is more flow and things seem to happen easily and naturally, even spontaneously. We seem to heal faster, age less, regenerate and even sometimes rejuvenate our bodies and cells and all sorts of possibilities are possible when we begin to nourish ourselves. Eating good organic foods and drinking spring water and such things are important but only go so far. Real nourishment comes from loving yourself and living from love. Allowing your energy to come forth.

When we love ourselves, our choices reflect our inherent self-worth and amazing things start to happen. The world around us changes. Relationships, finances, perspectives are altered.

Now, life can be a roller coaster ride and when you are experiencing circumstances that you do not desire and want to change it is an amazing opportunity to love yourself. Do not love yourself despite this or that – it is not "I love myself even though my boss fired me and my dog died" or "I love myself despite my big nose and feet" – No, choose to love yourself in your entirety, including your flaws and weaknesses and all, as otherwise your are blocking the flow of your energy and creating more limits.

The energy you are is not limited to any particular situation or circumstance.

Love energy encompasses all of creation, the "good" and the "bad". All choices, all movements. And in choosing to appreciate yourself you will give yourself the flexibility to move in any direction.

Choose your beingness.

A Question Worth Pondering

What is your relationship with time and space?

(and when you think you have it figured out, keep going)

Where Do You Think It All Comes From?

You can travel the world several times over.

You can travel the deserts and seas and cities and towns and villages of this little planet and behold it all.

You can journey to the farthest reaches of space where the universe has life forms and creations that your imagination cannot even comprehend.

You can create amazing things in your life and experience so much.

But don't forget that it is all the journey of you.

~The journey of you discovering you~

and moving deeper into awareness.

Open yourself to the interconnection and oneness of existence. As seeing yourself as separate from anything or everything is getting a little boring, isn't it?

And you have everything to explore.

Every choice out of fear

is a denial

of who you truly are.

The Illusion of Fear

When you feel fear try to observe what is really happening.

What I have learned about fear is that it is not real.

It is not what I am actually looking at that causes the fear and problems but *my own perception and reaction to something I do not like – ultimately something internal.*

Fear is a reflection of where you are at and what is inside of you. Nothing else.

It is a reflection of how you see yourself. Of how you are choosing to see yourself. In this regard it can serve you and be your friend.

And it is not easy to look unflinchingly at yourself and take responsibility for your choices.

But that is where our true freedom lies.

It is possible to reframe how you see any situation or circumstance and empower yourself.

Realize that there is no separation of anything in existence.

The world is your reflection, your playground.

Choice is your empowerment.

And you are the energy of choice.

Find Your Clarity

It wasn't until I said "thank you" and left all the books and learning and spiritual teachings behind that I started really connecting with myself.

That was when I found my clarity.

It is not until you start choosing for yourself and choosing you and connecting with that place within that you truly find yourself.

Be your own guide. Find your own truth. Trust in who you are and live your life.

Love and love some more and let everything else go.

There is nothing you need to learn that is not part of you already.

The View from a Ferris Wheel

"I see nothing in space as promising as the view from a Ferris wheel."

-E.B. White

Do you want to touch the infinite and explore the universe?

Start by touching and connecting with what is in front of you. Yourself and your life.

That is the only way you will get there.

Unspoken

My grandpa was born the year the Titanic sunk. In 1912.

I was born in 1976.

Growing up as a boy we used to spend time together, often in silence. Unspoken communication. Just enjoying the simplicity of being together. Small-town Saskatchewan.

Sometimes I would help him roll his cigarettes and watch in delight the dance of smoke drift upward and dissipate as it expanded into the room.

Sometimes I have regretted not talking more with him, asking him questions. About his life and what he learned in life.

But I know that in the silence we shared, everything was communicated. All the answers to any question I could have asked and more.

The love.

My relationship with my father is much the same.

Real communication is not with words.

Energy and the Perspective of Lineality

The energy you are is not limited to a point in space and time.

Observe how your energy interacts with your environment.

With the plants and people and even the building you live in.

Observe your ideas, thoughts and choices manifest into and as your life.

Observe how the energy you are extends into the future and past as well.

Time is not linear like it is commonly viewed.

And neither are you.

Observe what is around you. Observe yourself and allow your perspective to open.

Ask yourself what it truly means that you are not limited to one point or body in space and time.

Life Design

Every moment of your life is an expression (or lack of expression) of who you are.

Your energy and choices create your life regardless of who you are or the life you live.

So, begin with where you are.

What would you like to create?

Change the paradigm in which you live, the very rules in which you live by. If you want. Or play in the box you currently live in. Your worldview. Your perspectives. Be aware of your choices and explore new directions.

You are free to change jobs, change careers, change relationships. You are free to deepen your existing relationships or explore the relationship of all things.

What is it you truly want? It is important to begin with you. Your internal landscape. Your energy and state of being. Everything else will flow from there.

Your Beingness

Your beingness, your brilliance, is the expression of all that you are.

And that has nothing to do with trying or effort. It has nothing to do with trying to figure anything out or control anything.

It is simply about being you. The expression of All that you are.

And this expression isn't about shouting off the rooftops or from some pulpit (although it doesn't necessarily exclude that). It isn't about the way you dress or the money in your wallet. It isn't about how others see you or your needing approval from anyone or for anyone to see you a certain way. It isn't about any one particular expression either and it certainly is not about being cemented into a set of circumstances you do not like.

Your expression is about all that you are. You could say your beingness encompasses any way you could choose to manifest yourself.

Your beingness is simply you.

Look as far as you can see. Look to the horizon. Look to the stars and galaxies above. Look within the most advanced microscope at particles within particles within the atomic structure of our physicality...

...gaze upon your life. See how you live and the choices you make. See it for what it is...

...see everything around you. The movement and stillness and form and space of everything. Even the perspective you have of how time affects your environment, your physicality…

…observe your relationships. See how your choices create your relationships. See how your choices create your life…

Now, do you really think that you are separate from anything? You cannot draw a line anywhere in existence and say "This is energy, and this over here on this side is not." Everything is energy.

The energy that you are extends into everything.   Such is your sufficiency.

Open yourself up and explore what this means to you.

As the Madonna song says, "Express yourself."

You are infinitely worth it.

Are You Aware your Limits are Chosen?

Do you really feel that life ends when the body you have ceases to be? Do you believe in your heart that the essence and energy you are can ever cease to be?

You are life without beginning or end.   You are eternal, if you want to look at it from the judgment and filter of time. You are infinite.   You are energy.   And yes, you are manifested here, in this time-space reality.   But are you aware of all this?

The limits you exist by does not change who you truly are.

This life you are living, realize the theme of it is to experience and explore this idea of physicality and all that it entails. The intensity, density, limits and joy of it.

This physicality is not the summation of life but only an extension and representation of that which you are.   The energy and wonder and brilliance of you. So play with it and live large. Experience your empowerment and awakening.

Realize the You-consciousness that made the choice and continues to choose to be here now in the form and perception of you as you define yourself to be.

And realize what allows this choice.

Is Your Life Out of Balance?

Quit being busy. Quit that incessant need to do-do-do, go-go-go. It is a disease that will kill you faster than smoking.

Busyness is not your business and has nothing to do with productivity or living well.

Busyness has nothing to do with enjoying life or loving the self.

Busyness is not a way to create what you want in life but will actually keep you from what you want.

Understand the mindset that is involved in being busy. Observe the energy of it. Working "hard" is not a formula for success but a reflection of a lack perspective and a pushing for achievement.

Get comfortable being quiet with yourself and set up time for pause in your life. Cultivate breathing and relaxation as habits. In this moment there is nowhere to go and nothing to do.

Step out of the influence of your perceptions. Stop trying to please others or live in a way that is no longer serving you. Stop seeing yourself as a victim at the mercy of everything external to yourself, including "time", work, the weather, relationships, money, etc..

Take back your power. It simplifies everything.

Anyone who ever created anything worthwhile did so from their creative essence, their energy. Despite what it might look like.

When you come from your beingness, things will happen on their own.

Imagination

Imagination is not just a tool or aspect you can access and use in your life. Ultimately imagination is what you are. Creative energy. Essence.

Your life is created from imagination and fuels its expansion. The expansion of You. Do you see how it all works?

It is possible to shift your perspective and definition of who and what you think you are and choose more.

Never Stop Exploring

"Once you stop learning you start dying." – Einstein

Learning, asking questions, living, breathing, playing, growing, getting our hands dirty, aching belly laughs and funny faces.

These are things that keep us young and allow life energy to flow and infuse into our lives.

Never stop exploring.

Never stop using your imagination and bringing it into your life.

Question:

What is the relationship between learning and imagination?

The Seasons of Life and Change

One of the great things about living in Canada is that you really get to experience each of the four seasons in all their fullness. And each day has nuance and subtle shifts.

And such is our lives. There will be times when nothing seems to be going right and times when everything seems to flow like magic.

I ran into a friend recently that I hadn't seen in many months and after some conversation he mentioned that he ran into a whole host of different nasty health issues that took up a lot of his time and energy. But now he was doing better and, with his sense of humor and fun perspective of life, was looking forward to a better flow of things. He was waking up to the realization that life has those cycles and the importance of proper perspective.

And those of you who have experienced the bad and dark times when it looked like everything was collapsing and your life was imploding... haven't you always survived? And more than survived but gone on to enjoy life again?

When it seems darkest just remember that the sun is coming soon.

By observing nature and the flow of seasons, in whatever part of the world you are in, as well as everything around you, it is possible to get in touch with the impermanent and transient nature of reality. The illusion that it is. And so when shit comes up in life we can address it with an understanding that allows us calm and we are not easily thrown off balance.

And when you observe what changes, you will get a sense of something which is consistent and so broad that it underlies all the structure you have set up and designed your life as.

Every Moment

Every moment is an opportunity. Every moment is a choice.

Whatever you are doing whether it is eating, walking, sitting, working, playing, having sex, showering, watching TV, every moment is an opportunity to bring awareness into your life. Some people refer to it as mindfulness.

Every moment is an opportunity to bring space and ease into your existence

Observe how you are breathing or not breathing. Observe the tension in your body. Observe your mental and emotional state. Observe how you are feeling and how your life is flowing or constricted. In a general sense, observe how you interact with the world around you and how the world interacts with you.

See and feel the energy of what is happening.

Be Your Own Guru

How far do you think you will get in your spiritual journey when you put anyone or anything above yourself?

The great teachers like Buddha and Jesus and others taught a radical equality: *That they are not separate from you.*

But no one is willing to see and choose that type of limitless perspective. As it would mean moving past their fears and walls and blocks and comfortable belief systems and structured existence. It would mean moving past ideas of separation.

Everywhere now you see people giving their power away to everyone and anything outside of themselves — not just to religion or gurus but to their families, partners, bosses, antiquated belief systems, political correctness, societal expectations and rules/norms, to anyone who is richer, dresses better or who they perceive as smarter than they are. It is endless – observe it.

The hardest part of the journey of self-exploration is taking ownership of your own life and choices with a radical and complete honesty and commitment.

The spiritual journey becomes so complete that you will eventually extend your energy to become one with the All-That-Is. You will start to move in that direction at least.

And it is a process in which not one stone in the universe will be left untouched.

The next time you see a teacher sitting on a pedestal, whether it be tangible or subtle, observe what is happening and how it relates to you. The next time your mind makes a judgment of someone in relation to you, no matter what it is, observe it for a moment.

The games of existence are endless as well.

If you are not consciously choosing you, then you will be imbalanced and needy. And how can you be of benefit to anyone?

There is no teacher greater than you. Stop looking outside yourself.

You are that which you seek.

Explore What is Possible

You are caught up with your illusions.

Do you choose to move beyond them?

Create a movement in your life and explore that.

Open yourself up, be vulnerable and explore universal mysteries.

Explore 'the more' that you are.

and create a life that you can say:

"I finally woke up".

From Self-Help to Self-Love

I think my first 'self-help' book was in the form of a little offering at a Safeway cash register when I was a young boy. It was on meditation and I loved it even though it was "how-to" form oriented.

As a young teenager I read Napoleon Hill and Anthony Robbins and many others which were interesting but I didn't get much out of that whole genre. In a sense even the ***Tao Te Ching*** is a self-help book really. Eventually I read thousands of books, searching, exploring, always looking for that elusive something I was trying to connect with and remember.

But it wasn't in a book where I found what I was looking for.

And it wasn't in any teaching.

It was within me. It was me.

I was using books as a way **not** to connect with myself. It was a waiting period (that lasted for many years). Books only pointed to a direction, and most didn't even do that. Books can only go so far in what they give to us (including this one). Years ago, I gave away all of my books and only read for pleasure now.

And that is why I kept my book **Ayama's Journey: The Nature of Reality** short and used a story to communicate what I wanted to express and share with the world.

To begin the journey of self-discovery is simply to appreciate and love yourself. When we are ready and choose, it all begins.

This Isn't About Navel-gazing

Don't worry about saving the world. Save yourself.

If you want to be of service to the world, your family or yourself, then realize it's not your actions so much that will amount to much (if anything).

It is your quality and state of being that matters.

The energy that you are.

That is what makes lasting ripples.

This is a world bent and torn on self-destruction and harm.

It does not need another ego-personality running around doing stupid shit.

You cannot make another person choose or do anything. Not really.

Besides, isn't really boring at this point trying to control things?

So, take care of being the best version of you that you can be and allow the universe to just be.

One Shift in Consciousness

One shift in your consciousness

does more for the world

than one hundred lifetimes of philanthropy.

How is this so?

Because you are moving past the level where the problem
arises.

And you are not separate from anything.

So live and play and create and assist others if you choose.
Build those schools in Malawi. Support cancer research.
Volunteer at the local shelter.

But realize that to move into real and lasting change you
need to create from the energy that is you.

The Choice that Heals

The main thing I know about healing is that is requires choosing. Maybe that is the only thing that I know about it really, but it is enough.

A year back I had injured a rib and it was one of those annoying injuries that affects your mobility. And I was trying to not let it affect my life too much and one day doing my simple yoga routine in the park I was shifting into Trikonasana (Triangle Pose) and my injured rib went CRACK! as I lifted my arm above my head to the sky. I felt my rib or something snap.

Well that's what I got for not really listening to my body.

The rib injury was much more acute now and greatly affected my movement. It was lingering for weeks. And one day I realized that I had experienced it enough and did not want to anymore.

And in a moment I made a choice to heal and simultaneously felt the rib shift. The healing was instant and complete.

And it did not require a touch or anything. Just a choice. But in that choice was a clarity and definiteness. An ease. In fact, the Asymya I did on it in the preceding days did not do much for it because underlying the energy work there wasn't the full choice to shift and heal. I was sort of just going through the motions.

Choosing connects us back with our power. It is our empowerment. It is not anything or anyone outside of yourself that heals you. Only you can heal you. And really, would you want it any other way?

Healing is a topic that leads to a discussion of the oneness of things.

And there is everything to explore in existence, is there not?

You Are the Exploration

Growing up in Saskatchewan there was a lot of space. Not just to move around but to reflect and contemplate existence.

Regina was not a big city (you could drive across it in 10 minutes by car) and there was a slow pace to life – even more so in the country where the wheat fields stretch out to horizon and the wind creates waves and sway like the ocean.

Some of the most memorable and happiest times of my life have been the space of just existing, being alive and feeling the vastness yet interconnection of everything. Where everything starts flowing together and you are aligned with the deeper energy of things and infuse yourself into that movement.

It's like going to an amusement park. You have to choose to go on the ride and then buckle up.

If you pay attention, the universe is speaking to you, nodding and nudging, whispering, asking and begging to play and create with and through you but you have to listen carefully.

In your interaction with anything or anyone, even yourself you can create a movement.

You can feel the 'more'. The interconnection and oneness.

Being a Seeker is Not a Bad Thing

With a true seeker there is an honesty and openness to see and connect deeper. There is a desire to move beyond the limits of one's life into a deeper awareness and movement, into the remembrance of what is.

But a seeker will remain seeking until the choice is made to realize themselves and to no longer deny what they are. The danger of seeking is not moving past the role or game of it. It becomes a way of life, a way of "I am not ready or worthy" at the psychological level.

Paradoxically, seeking can be a way of not moving deeper into yourself, of not owning your choices. A perpetual justification and denial of one's self.

In Every Student is a Great Teacher

What is your expression in the world?

What kind of example do you wish to be to everyone and everything around you?

Your energy ripples out into the universe and touches everything.

Let your greatest offering, your greatest teaching, *be that which you are*.

Your beingness encompasses everything.

So do not limit yourself. Do not limit your expression.

Exploring the New Paradigm

Are you interested in self-growth, self-exploration?

These concepts of sufficiency, of empowerment, of energy, understand they will lead you to the realization of who you are. The shift will not be sideways to explore from the structure you have adopted and established for yourself but an entirely new way of seeing the world. It will be a new paradigm. A new way of existing.

As you open to a new awareness of things the world around you changes from being an external environment to one where you realize everything is an extension of you. A reflection of you and your perceptions. Energy is consciously extended 'outward' and this movement is internal as well. Every internal movement and realization reflect into your reality.

Understand, these concepts of internal, external and movement, time and growth, etc. only exist as we insist on seeing ourselves and everything with filters, with judgment.

Imagine living in this new way... knowing that you and everything around you is energy. That you are not separate from anything. A practical result of this would be to move through 'time' without a loss or dissipation of energy. You would live longer and not age the way everyone does. As a result of your choices your life would become easier, more joyful, richer... imagine the possibilities.

Basically, it comes down to choice. That is your power. That is your ability.

What do you choose to explore?

Opening

What is your awareness of yourself?

What is the story and role you have created your life to be?

How have you given your power away to everything and everyone else?

What is the vision of yourself and your life you want to live and be?

What choices would you have to make to bring that into your reality?

What is your awareness of existence and your relationship with everything you perceive?

Why do you consistently choose to see yourself as separate from everything around you?

What is the larger movement of your life and the flow of lifetimes you manifest yourself as?

What are your daily choices?

What is your choice in this very moment?

Open to the realization of what you are.

Beautiful, Sexy, Amazing

It is not the physical look of a person that makes them truly sexy, beautiful and attractive.

It is their energy and how they see themself.   Their relationship with themself and how they appreciate and love themself and how this energy extends outward into the world.

Do you see yourself as beautiful, sexy, amazing, talented, intelligent and attractive?   Do you appreciate these qualities within yourself? If you cannot, how is anyone else going to see you? How are you going to manifest the life you truly want to be living if you do not appreciate who you are, all of your qualities, your essence?

Stand in front of a mirror and see what is there. Do not turn away but explore your relationship with yourself. Get naked and be real with yourself. Be willing to ask and answer the tough questions.

It is Not Impossible to Dream Real

Imagine this: you wake up one morning and the world you see is totally different, totally new. While you were sleeping you gained an awareness that bubbled up from your subconscious mind and stayed with you into your waking reality.

You wake up and you feel an intense vibrancy and vitality. There is an ease and joy and connectedness with all those around you and everything in your environment. Everything feels alive and the energy you are extends itself into everything you perceive such that nothing is separate from you.

Imagine the possibilities...

Form and Flow

Do not worry about appearances.

Do not worry about the form your message will take or what you will say or how your expression will look.

Do not try to package or make your product or service or expression shine.

Just being who you are is everything. And it is enough.

Moving Beyond the Influence of Your Perceptions

"Seeing is believing, but sometimes the most real things in the world are the things we can't see."
                    -The Conductor in the movie Polar Express

Life is a dream.

But your perceptions will give you 'evidence' otherwise.

How far will you choose to see?

How far will you choose to explore in your life?

How far will you open yourself up?

The thing about limitlessness is that it goes far beyond what is physical.

Perception is an interesting thing.

Choice

The choices you make ripple out into the world and universe and extend throughout time.

They literally alter, and are, the fabric of existence.

The Larger Perspective

The universe is big place. We actually have to use our imagination to even start to comprehend the scale and size of it.

(A related topic is how imagination informs reality.)

The only comparison is the infinite world of sub-atomic particles which is equally as vast. Ultimately you can say they are the same thing.

And within all of this is the point in space and time in which you exist. Your physicality, your life, your perception and awareness of things. Your awareness of you.

Realize something important here. Everyone has an "environmental situation" in which they live and in which they are born into. The essence you are chose to be here. And chooses to be here. And it is you here right now making choices that determines what your life is and will become.

That is a powerful idea and can become your awareness.

It is the opposite of the victim mentality that exists in the world today.

Living in awareness will open you to different ways of living that will expand and grow your existence.

How Far are You Willing to Open Yourself?

You will reach a point on your journey when all the

self-doubt

self-definitions

and self-imposed limits

you exist by will become frustrating and boring.

And it is then you will start to let go of who and what you think you are.

You will let go of what you think your life is and should be.

And it is here you will open to realize

what love truly is.

Be What You Will

Be a success. Be a failure. Be rich. Be poor.

Be bold. Be timid. Be open. Be closed.

Be hard. Be soft. Be a visionary. Be myopic.

Be a rock star. Be a nobody.

Run along and swim naked in the ocean. Or build your sand castles on the shore.

Be a sinner. Be a saint. Be sexual. Be nonsexual. Live long. Die young.

Fly high. Stay grounded. Love. Hate.

Be afraid. Be fearless.

Live your life. Change how you see yourself. Be who you want to be. Make mistakes. It is okay.

It is more than okay. It is inevitable. And from one perspective there are no mistakes.

Explore what is possible. You might surprise yourself.

It's Okay to Feel

It's more than okay — it's being honest with yourself.

It's okay to feel hurt, fearful, angry, jealous, happy, despair, etc. And you can allow that. The mind does not have to control or protect you from your feelings.

Embrace your feelings. If it is something strong, feel the fire of it, the intensity. The fullness and depth. And that way you can acknowledge and not deny any part of yourself.

When we allow ourselves to truly feel we then become free to live in the moment and not carry with us the baggage from the past. As it will be released. We become free to tell a new story and set a new direction in our lives if we choose.

Life is about what happens now, what we experience in the moment.

This Life is a Dream

The brook flows.

Come, sit by the water's edge. Feel the coolness and hear the trickle. Relax into its shimmering beauty. Allow your senses to bask in the pleasure of it as you release any concerns of your day.

Open and allow your energy to relax. Take a few deep breaths.

The world and everyone and everything in it are reflections of what is inside of you. The face you see in the mirror everyday is not your reflection — the world is.

The world is your mirror, your reflection. A reflection of your perception, thoughts, movement, judgments, choices, imagination, desire, creative energy, psychologies and more. Not the totality of that which you are but it does reflect.

Pause for a moment and see this.

You are living this dream called life. And so is everyone else.

This is not something to get caught up about. It's a rather funny and amusing thing if you think about it. We incarnate here and experience physical existence. It is something to enjoy and play with.

Put your feet in the water and splash around a little. Get comfortable and explore new terrain. See what opens up and experience new fears. And move beyond it.

The clouds reflect off the surface of the brook. The air fills your lungs. Feel your energy extend to encompass everything.

Be in Wonder Again

Appreciate your life and everything in it.

Do not take anything too seriously.

Remember when you were a boy or girl and used to look up to the sky and twirl around and fall to the ground all dizzy and joyful?

Remember seeing the newness and wonder of it all and were exploring it, discovering where the boundaries were?

Maybe it is time to explore and play again and to discover new boundaries and limits.

Be in wonder again.

Be joyful.

Smile.
Play.
Laugh.
Make Love.
Hold each other.
Fall in love again.
Fall in love with yourself and your life.

Challenge yourself to see things in new ways.

Walk barefoot in the water, sand and grass.

Greet a stranger like they were your best friend or share compliments more freely.

Dare yourself to be a little crazy.

Revel in the monotony when it arises at your job and imagine new possibilities.

Sing a song that you love or write a new one.

Buy the person behind you in line a coffee.

Inspire a new movement in the world or in yourself.

Being more alive doesn't mean jumping out of planes or free climbing up vertical rock faces or putting your life in danger. It's about opening up your horizon and being who you are already at the core but have forgotten.

Get in touch with your essence, your energy.

Give thanks to the universe.   Extend your energy in appreciation and love.

there is magic in every single moment
with every single breath.

Life is Everywhere

Life is the trees and grass you move by.

It is the magpies as they look up at you and chirp.

It is the rain and water and clouds and sky.

It is in the sun and stars and infinite reaches of space in which this little planet is less than a speck.

It is the smile of children and loved ones but also the expressionless millions that walk and bus and drive to work each morning.

It is in that creep who gave you an unwanted smile.

It is the creative energy it took to construct the dwellings and cityscape you live in.

It is your relationships and desires and imagination and movement.

It is the love and lack of love you have for yourself.

It encompasses your expansions and contractions throughout life. Your smiles and sorrow and all.

It is the creative impetus that gave rise to life here and everywhere.

It is the choice you made to be here now. To come into physical existence the way you have, isn't it?

Life is everywhere. It is what we experience, what we create, what we choose. It is You.

See it.

Feel it.

You are the energy of life. The essence of existence.

Are you not?

Peace of Mind

"You cannot find peace by avoiding life." -Virginia Woolf

Everybody seems to be looking for it.

This thing called "peace". Peace of mind. Whatever you want to call it.

I was playing some blitz chess yesterday and a chess player I hadn't seen for some years showed up. It was a nice surprise as he is an affable guy who is an amateur boxer. I asked him how his training is going and he said he is "training to find peace".

And that is where it all starts, isn't it? Being aware of what you want and where you are at.

Ms. Woolf's quote about peace is quite astute.

You cannot find peace by building yourself a nice little box or worldview and living inside that. You cannot find peace by trying to control your life or protect yourself from the world. Quite the opposite. *A certain degree of vulnerability is required.*

And vulnerability is a choice to move into and express your beingness in the world.

I have found that the times in my life which have been the most devoid of "peace" are when I am not expressing myself: the situation or person I am reacting to and allowing a contraction of my energy.

Peace implies the opposite of something. The opposite of war or conflict or whatever. And that is not really what we all want is it? As just because it is not raining problems or you are not being triggered by something/someone does not mean you have achieved anything real or lasting, does it?

It is not really a peace of mind we want but an expression of who we are.   That energy. As our beingness is a state of ease.   It is state of vitality and our natural energy.   An awareness.

Moving into your vulnerability will bring you closer to what you are seeking.

And that is a choice.

Small is a Good Thing

Small can sometimes be a good thing.

On your journey through life you will experience life and there will be shifts in your understanding of things.

If will usually not be a "Eureka!" moment but a series of small shifts. Real-ize here these shifts do add up. Eventually they add up to a lot.

And they prepare the way for larger shifts in awareness. Into awareness. Each choice you make paves the way for new choices and further exploration of yourself and existence.

One day you will look in the mirror and there will be a completely different person standing there. Perhaps an earlier vision you had of yourself.

Inherent in the smallness of things is the opening into everything else.

A largeness beyond imagination.

You are that which You Seek

The oneness that you are

the oneness of existence

encompasses your perspectives of separation.

It encompasses your limits and every choice.

What do you think love is?

Everything that is

or that could possibly be

is encompassed, supported and infused by something

that you are not separate from.

Be a Lover

It's easy to be hard.

It's easy to be tough.

It's easy to be a killer and destroy things (including yourself).

It's easy to put up a wall around your heart and try to protect yourself.

But it's also a losing game.

Be vulnerable.

Be you.

Your Vision of You

I found myself feeling overwhelmed recently.

I was juggling many different and new things for weeks and some toxic stuff was happening at work. The specifics of that are not important for things always pop up in life that can pull us from our state of being.

And I shifted back into my preferred state of being by asking a simple question:

What is the (highest/boldest) vision you have of yourself?

It is a powerful question as immediately it opens up the field of possibility and imagination and facilitates an awareness of where we are now and what our current choices are. It connects you with your passions.

In other words, where would you like to be? What directions would you like to explore? Think about! Wonder about! Feel it! What is the highest vision of you that you would like to connect with, choose, create and experience?

Shifting states is something you can do in a moment, or very quickly. With practice, by being aware it is possible to instantly upshift to an empowered state of being. Remember, you are the energy of possibility and can move in any direction, as you so choose. Can you not?

Awareness is a practice to shift deeper into awareness.

Awareness is our natural place of being and more.

<h1 style="text-align:center">State of Mind</h1>

If you are not feeling good, recognize the influence of your mind on your life.

In fact, if you are not feeling great observe how the mind is interfering in your existence.

Acknowledge how you are feeling. Observe the discord or disharmony or lack of ease in your life. Do not deny this or it will perpetuate itself.

To be conscious and embrace the fullness of who you are the mind must be guided to a larger realization of things. And this is not easy. It will likely be the hardest thing you ever do, when you are ready to go in that direction. For it will mean that you are no longer willing to allow the mind free reign to contract or reduce your life.

The interesting thing is that the mind is part of who we are. It is not something separate from us. But it must be directed. Commanded. Guided. For it will otherwise go in a direction that is likely not of your choosing and will be to your detriment. Observe this and you will see it. Any perception of lack is a reflection of the mind's limited perspective. And any perception can be shifted.

(realize the influence of your perceptions on your life!)

When there is stress or a lack of ease in your life recognize that there is a battle going on. The mind is trying to run your life and is like a bully or child.

That is why a regular practice of meditation or energy work or even doing something you enjoy like working out or dancing is such a good idea. It can facilitate an opening to the bigger picture.

Guide your mind so that it knows its place. Make it your ally on your journey of life. It is an amazing and powerful tool, far beyond what is commonly understood.

The Perception of Time

This movement that you call your life.

This passage of time.

Consider what time really is.

Consider that it is much more than you have thought it is.

Feel this river of 'life' and experience.

You perceive a movement, a perspective of change and growth and decline.

And you name it. You call it time.

(And everything is therefore measured, judged and controlled.)

Beyond this perspective what else could "time" truly be?

And what would it mean to open yourself to something beyond the influence of your perceptions?

Observe. This is a direction your mind will quickly steer away from.

Challenge Your Perceptions

It could be the image of the iris of an eye. Or a picture of a blue sun. Or a new universe. Or the image of a sub-atomic particle. Or a swimming pool. Or something else.

Always challenge what you see. Challenge your perceptions.

The world is a big place. And not so big.

Shift your perceptions to see the larger picture when the mind tries to contract your existence.

Reframe your perspective if you ever find yourself in a situation you do not like.

Be aware of your choices is life and your movement through existence.

Explore how you see yourself and the world.

Your physicality is not an absolute.

Do You Accept this Dare?

Each and every human being is an expression of the
brilliance of all that is.

No matter who they are.

Life is an energy of choice. And we are that energy of choice.

Redefine yourself if you dare.

In some new and expansive way.

Parable: The Boy and the Ocean

There was a boy who lived by the ocean waters. He learned to fish for a living (as his father had before him) and lived a simple life.

And he lived his life from joy and love and because of that lived a rich life and all of his needs were met. More than met. And some saw him as a teacher or master even though he did not speak much.

Inside of himself he maintained and allowed to grow, an awareness of himself connected with all of existence.

The movement of his energy was such that he realized the ocean was within himself.

He realized his sufficiency within existence.

"Don't Try"

These two words are the epitaph of the poet Charles Bukowski (1920-1994). He lived a hard life and struggled but came to a certain understanding within himself.

He played a role (and knew it). A few different ones in his lifetime. We all do.

I admire him for his ability to see the world. And despite his hard ways there was a gentleness inside of him that he let come out.

There is a power when we let go of the struggle and trying to uphold the bullshit of our lives. Not just the stress and roles but carrying around anything and everything that is not us.

Letting go is simplicity itself. Easy, no. It will be the hardest thing you ever achieve.

Embrace the inner sight of the poet in you and see through the illusions of the world. The illusions you have created for yourself.

And the next time you drink beer or wine, give a nod to C.B. No wiser words were ever written then the two etched on his gravestone.

The Benefits of Meditation

The benefits are many and varied, of course. That goes without saying and I won't list them all here. (Physical, emotional and mental well-being are at the top of the list.)

Meditation is not about having epiphanies or grand realizations that immediately lead to enlightenment (however you want to define that).

Meditation is about the daily choice and consistency that you give to yourself to support your movement into a deeper understanding and awareness.

And there will be shifts in your awareness. Greater clarity will naturally arise and you will realize things like:

"Oh yeah, I do try to control my relationship with X and I don't have to. In fact, it is limiting things and damaging (in a way I did not see before)."

or

"I have been trying so hard to accomplish X and I don't have to. I can easily accomplish what I want to do by allowing it to happen. The work has been done and I can get out of the way."

or

"Here is a new idea or clarity about X that I never had before. "

And it will effortless and natural. There will be a shift in perception and thinking arising from a greater awareness of reality.

Meditation is about embracing more ease into your life. An ease based on the observation and knowing of who you are.

And the daily choice to meditate is a choice that will lead to wonderful and amazing things and support you in your life.

The Value of Having a Mind
(For Those Who Haven't Lost Theirs) ...

The value is that you can be conscious.

You can consciously direct your mind and use it as the tool that it is.

You can tell it to go in any direction... *of your choosing*.

And if that isn't empowerment then what is?

One example of directing the mind is to give it this idea:

"I choose to be more open and see what the universe brings to me."

(And then, observe what new opportunities that arise and what doors are opened. And beyond that, to observe the abundance of the universe and your relationship with all things.)

Going Deeper

Just when you believe that you are being honest and real with yourself...

that you have looked at your fears and judgments...

that you have observed your perspectives of insufficiency and lack...

that you have looked in the mirror and asked the tough questions such as "Do I truly love myself?" ...

that you have looked at emotional "issues" such as anger, resentment, etc.

that you have become aware of underlying tensions in your life (and body) ...

understand then, at that moment, there is a space to go further and deeper...

to be truly honest with yourself.

You can justify any choice. The justification process can be almost endless and can move through many lifetimes. Or you can simple choose. And the choice we are talking about here is one of empowerment.

It is a choice that will move you to the next phase of your journey.

No Rules to this Journey

There are no rules to this game.

The exploration of yourself and existence.

And sure that is exciting and scary.

But would you want it any other way?

An Experiment

Imagine for a moment that the distance between yourself and any object is just a thought.

A perception.

Consider the "time" it takes to move somewhere or do something.

Consider the inter-relationship between time and the perception of space.

Now, play with this element called time. Is it possible to shift this perception, to shift it such that the distance and time it takes to be somewhere or complete a task no longer exists?

What would this mean to your existence?

Is it possible that the experience that you call your life...that it all began with a thought?

A simple extension of energy, your energy?

This is where the creative essence of the universe exists. This place within you.

You are the creative essence.

Listening to Your Own Voice

When I was 20, I remember sitting at the library and tackling the formidable book **I AM That** by Nisargadatta Maharaj.

I wanted to understand it as I felt there was something important in it but it was no use as I didn't have a frame of reference or spiritual vocabulary for it yet.

And then when I was 30, I tried it again and understood it.

And I found it interesting that another of India's famous modern gurus, the soft-spoken Ramana Maharshi, essentially taught the same thing and had opposite personalities. Where one shouted the other sat in silence with little reliance on words.

And over years I read the teachings and offerings of hundreds of teachers and books committed to finding that elusive integration and truth of everything. It took a while as I was not going within consistently. I was searching and exploring externally even though most of the teachings pointed to the same place.

And, of course, there is no shortage of gurus in the world. There are no shortages of religion or people who are more than happy to tell you how to live or get enlightened. And generally, that is what people want: they want the truth sugar-coated, sexy, elusive, and they want it watered down.

For when you go digging for the truth of existence, you will meet your fears. Fears that you didn't even know existed. A mountain bigger and badder than Everest in the worst snow storm.

The short of it is that we fear our own brilliance.

Always remember: the answers are inside of you. Everyone intuitively knows that to be true. But living that way is another story. Imagine what would happen if you became your own compass and made your choices with the trust that you are exploring you.

Realizing who you are is like freediving. You hold your breath and give up everything to go deep and find that one pearl.

Choose the Role You Want to Play

Tell a different story.

You are not the 25-year-old unemployed college grad with a mountain of debt and no boyfriend.

You are not the 82-year-old retiree waiting on death's door.

You are not the burned out single-parent mother working two jobs.

You are not the bored CEO or business owner trapped in a role that doesn't reflect anything about you.

You are not your story.

Reinvent yourself.

Tell a different story.

Or you can just be you.

In the moment.

Observe and realize that you are not in a static reality. Even though it is often perceived that way (and accepted), play around and open to the flexibility of what your existence can be.

It all begins and ends with you. Your choices.

What do you think is the energy behind the universe and the creation you call your life?

Integrity

Integrity: 'the state of being whole and undivided'.

What does that mean for you in your life?

I came across a quote recently that was along the lines that described integrity as the path in which you will never lose yourself.

From a spirituality perspective having integrity you might say is the commitment and choice to connect with the essence of yourself. Being whole.

As everything else is a fragmentation of the self or even an act of fraud and dishonesty. Isn't it?

From this perspective, for instance, integrity has nothing to do with morality. Concepts of right and wrong, good and bad are just adopted societal norms.

We are so used to playing our roles that I do not think that integrity is a very common thing at all.

The Importance of Pause

It is essential to have a daily practice of taking time out for yourself.

A practice in which you quiet the mind

connect deeper

and regenerate yourself.

This includes relaxation and deep breathing.

It can take any form such as: meditation, yoga, gardening, energy work, tai chi, running, walking or something else.

Or it can be as simple as sitting in a comfortable chair in a quiet room.

This habit will pay dividends far beyond anything the best stocks will.

It will give you more than you can possibly imagine (if you do it consistently over time).

Your Relationship with the World

It may seem obvious but it is worth thinking about:

You learn about who you are from your relationship with others.

You learn about who you are from your relationship with your

environment and circumstances.

(When things get tough, what is your choice?)

You learn about who you are and what is possible from your choices.

You learn about who you are from your relationship with yourself.

So, what is your relationship with yourself and everything?

What do you see yourself as separate from?

Moving Beyond 'How to' Methodologies

"The great home of the Soul is the open road."
-Walt Whitman

The 'how to' approach will only get you so far in life.

Like winning games or coming up with controlled strategies on getting what you want.

But in your movement to awaken to the more of what you are you will not get anywhere if you are not open and vulnerable and willing to relinquish the way you think things are or should be.

Universal energy will not flow through you if you are in a holding pattern or blocked.

Strategy and technique is for the game players. It is not for those who choose to see the world as it is and step out of the box.

The Mind Does Not Give Up So Easily

Like the overtired kid in the grocery store, the mind will kick and scream in attempts to regain some type of footing and control.

The key here is that the You that is you commands the mind. That deeper part of who you are.

In meditation and the practice of daily awareness, incrementally, you will guide and show the mind that it has an important role to play but it is no longer free to run the show.

Guide your mind to the understanding and awareness that control is an illusion, that reality is an illusion, and that what is real is not something that can be defined.

You cannot be the ocean if you are standing at the water's edge and afraid to jump in. Choose your direction and the mind will follow. It has no choice at that point.

And who does the choosing? Not the ego-personality but the essence you are.

Observe how the mind works. Accept its nature and appreciate it. For it is part of you.

Take that First Step

What does the choice for self-empowerment mean for you?

What does it feel like?

The energy of a choice is an energy of clarity.

It is a movement in a new direction.

A direction that you choose.

A direction that you want to explore and experience.

And self-empowerment is about taking back your power that you have given away to the beautiful illusion you call the world, the universe. The power that you have given away to virtually everything outside of yourself (including your own fears).

Your movement does not have to be one in which this is so.

In the grandest sense of exploration in existence even the immutable laws such as 'cause and effect' do not hold absolute sway over your choices. In a moment anything can happen (if you truly allow it).

Things are possible (and even probable) that you have not yet even begun to imagine for yourself.

Open yourself to possibility and take the first step.

Pick a Number Between 1 and 10

As a boy six or seven years old, I remember doing an experiment with my mom and sister.

We sat on the floor and rolled dice. It was for a research paper my mom was doing for a Psych class at the time and it became clear quickly that more than randomness was at play.

I told them that I was going to roll 3s with the set of dice and my sister did a similar thing and it soon became a statistical impossibility that luck was at play in the number of times a 3 was rolled. That is a fun memory.

But psychic ability is about much more than what the media tends to portray. It goes beyond merely finding lost keys or people communicating with a dead relative.

As awareness expands so does psychic ability. As it is an inner knowing of things. Nothing to get caught up about or blow the horn about.

Another example from my life is that I can look at a person and will just know things about them – from an energetic standpoint, and just know who they are and what their choices are.

That this ability even exists is a reflection of the oneness of existence. And it has been said many times — *you are not separate from anything* (even though it is one of the most popular games people play with themselves and others).

Real psychic ability is not a common thing at all even though it is often said that "anyone can become a psychic". That is not true. It is not true because it is simply not their choice (ie. to observe existence and see things as they are).

Real psychic ability is a byproduct of your movement and exploration of the oneness and interconnection of all things.

Cracking Open the Tool Shed

There is a way to open yourself up to everything that is.

It will open you to the limitlessness of existence.

It's a way that will dramatically change your perspectives and connect you with the deeper awareness of things.

It's represents a doorway to infinite possibility (and choice) and will take you as far as you want to go, if you let it.

And it's something that you will likely judge and dismiss in quick fashion. (As it is not sexy and doesn't have any bells or whistles or flashing lights and besides, it's scary moving into a radical new way of living.)

But if you explore it you will come to see just what a powerful tool it is as it allows you to guide your conscious mind into the realization that you no longer have to uphold your world together.

You can allow everything to be. And you can simply be.

And when you come to understand just what it means, maybe this tool will be exciting and sexy for you, in a sense. This tool is simply this:

Observation without judgment

Do you trust that the universe supports

your movement and choices?

Or, is it reflecting

your beliefs of scarcity and lack?

Living a 'Soul' Directed Life

When I was a boy and teenager, I never understood the term 'soul'. It made no sense. I came across it in either a religious or scholarly context that seemed abstract and removed from my life.

And it wasn't until many years later that the term "essence" or "soul-essence" finally clicked in and I realized what it was – that it was me, my true essence and energy that these terms refer to. The deeper part of yourself beyond the ego-personality role.

And that was a turning point for me. Because it meant that it was all eminently and infinitely practical. For me it was more real than the reality in which we give our power away to.

It meant that understanding of the universe and life was possible and that I could start to grow in understanding and awareness. It meant that I could start to live from that place.

And I am still exploring and choosing this in my life. It is a simple choice that drives my life and choices and I do not always come from that place but it has become easier over the years.

Connecting with that energy opens up so much because it is the energy of existence. That place which we are all one. And the choice is a consistency and broadening beyond anything else.

Love is what we are.

Moving Beyond Limiting Paradigms

One conversation that I avoid having with people is about the concept that there are no victims in the world.

Basically, what I tell the few that I broach the subject with is that there is only perception, choice and experience. Love. Very few are ready or interested in hearing about that because it means taking total ownership of yourself.

People seem to be offended when you challenge such a basic thing as their victim mindset is such an ingrained way of thinking, taught to everyone from infancy. They assume that is just how things are, almost as a badge of honor. People will site some example where a person or a group of people died through disease or acts of violence which were 'beyond their control'.

But what they do not realize is that there is no control of anything in existence. Control is just an illusion of your mind. Trying to control anything is like trying to force a shape with water or a tell a cat to do something. It is not possible. Sure things happen in life that make us sad, hurt and feeling pain. I am not diminishing that. I encourage people to acknowledge their feelings and acknowledge where they are at.

When I say that 'there are no victims in the world' that does not mean than we should disregard the environment in which we are in or do whatever we want. This is a world of cause and effect. If you choose to jump off a building you will suffer the effect of that. If you choose to give a gang member the finger you might find yourself with a problem. Some choices are more sustainable, healthier and life-affirming than others. We need to respect our world and each other and acknowledge our beliefs and belief systems.

It is important to realize that you chose, on a conscious level or not:

To be in the environment you are in.

To see the world and yourself the way you do.

To express yourself as you are.

These choices actively create the reality you experience. *And absolutely no one or thing can harm you unless you choose to allow it. Through your choices.*

Do you think the essence energy you are – the deeper self – chose to be here only to be thrown around by the tides and vicissitudes of random chaos? That is not how the universe works. Sure we experience the myriad of limits that is the human experience, but only until we open ourselves to more.

The human perspective is (currently) one of singular consciousness for the most part. We define ourselves as separate form everything around us. It becomes a way and form of disempowerment and it is impossible to live from a place of love when we live in a place of separation.   If we are separate from anything then it would make sense that we have to try to protect ourselves and devise strategies for survival, success, etc.

Having said that, to move beyond self-imposed limits it must be observed how 'fear' and 'separation' are parallel ideas. They reinforce each other. They are two sides of the same coin.

Compassion is impossible when we cannot see and choose from a perspective of what unites us.   *From the larger perspective there is only the energy of choice. Not even that.*

149 |The Inner Journey: A Guide to Awakening

Just choice. Just love. You can see and define yourself in any way you choose. Or you can live in a bubble and cry foul. That is your choice and you are free to choose whatever you wish. But you are more than your conscious mind. And ultimately your movement will be to open up to what is beyond 'single consciousness' perspectives.

It is possible to shift your perspective to see the brilliance of each human expression (regardless of what another's choice may be) and it begins with you. You will not be able to see the miracle of another if you do not see the miracle that is you. Your own brilliance. So that is a great practice for those who want to expand their lives.

We are all here to empower ourselves and to see through the illusion of things. A state of real empowerment is not trying to maneuver successfully and achieve a better, more secure position in the world. It is to move into your vulnerability and see that this world has no power over you. Power comes from who and what you are.

What is it that you choose in your life?

The Paradox of Problems

A problem often cannot be solved at the level or consciousness of the problem itself. The mind will keep spinning and the walls will remain.

But open yourself to more and realize that you can create a new structure or paradigm for your life. One that will present new limits and issues.

And the exploration will continue from there.

But ask yourself...

Are you here to solve problems?

Or, are you here for more?

An example from my own life w was when I was feeling stagnant with an old job and could not find a different one. So instead of 'trying harder' and getting frustrated, I went on a vacation to Jamaica and after that moved into a new job opportunity that was always there before (but I did not see it).

Shift your perspective and energy and allow the rest to fall into place. That is my approach to things, basically.

Limitless

From an absolute perspective, are there any consequences to choice if in each moment we are free to choose in any direction?

We perceive reality as a continuity of one moment into another, from one point in space-time to another. But that is a very limited perspective of what reality and existence truly is. A very linear one.

Open yourself to the awareness that you are choice. Choose and choose again, creating, exploring and experiencing yourself, never-ending.

And from that "point" wouldn't your life be a reflection of your limitlessness, despite and because of each choice you make?

In the Beginning

Some in the world are starting to open to the role that perception and choice have in creating reality.

What would it mean to observe time and reality for all that it is?

Would you believe that your life began with a thought?

What would it mean to observe yourself and everything around you and all that is at the point where it all began?

What would it mean to get in touch with that original perception that began it all?

Well, anything would be possible at that moment, wouldn't it?

Within the Heart of Everyone

Within the heart of everyone is love.

And love is everywhere.

That includes you.

You can see it in the space between your choices.

You can see it in the context of the choices you make, even when it is a choice to reduce yourself or harm another.

You can see it in the interconnection of things and how the universe supports our movement and choices.

There is nowhere you can walk or run or travel in the universe or in your imagination or within yourself where there is not love.

Love is the space within a cup that holds the water and the cup itself.

Love cannot be all of this and be something separate from who you are.

Love supports life and is what we are.

Why do you deny this at every step and actively play out a role and personality that is not a true reflection of you?

Why do you pretend that anything in this world has any real influence or some inherent ability to disempower or make you feel like shit?

That is good for a laugh my friends.

It is time to own up to things and be honest with yourself.

It is time to make a choice to explore things a bit deeper.

So, where would you like to go from here?

It is interesting to observe that the heart has an infinite capacity to love and that the universe has infinite possibilities to explore.   Hmmm, maybe there is a connection...:-)

A Good Traveler

"A good traveler has no fixed plans and is not intent upon arriving."

(ch. 27 Tao Te Ching)

This applies to traveling but also our way of being in the world. For we are all here as temporary visitors on this planet.

And I love this quote because it distills so much into a few words. If we are not prepared to be in each moment, living now and embracing what is before us and appreciating the universe, then do we ever really live?

We are explorers, living in the world and sometimes connecting with the deeper pulse of things. We are all travelers. Whether your idea of a travel is touring the Croatian coastline, hitchhiking across the prairies, or going to the fridge on a commercial break.

"Without going outside, you may know the whole world."

(ch. 47, Tao Te Ching)

And this verse is a kind of a sister passage to the previous one. For what we see in the world is ultimately a reflection of our own perception and understanding.

There will always be things happening in the world that will create fear in people.

It is up to you to align your life and choices in the direction you want to go.

When you resist anything doesn't it make sense that you are in fact just supporting it with your energy?

Don't give your power away to anything.

Stop resisting anything and start saying "Yes!" to what you do want and go in that direction. Even if you are the only one.

Yes, things are shaping up for some big events that will take place. Where many people will be affected and die. That is just the writing on the wall and it is plain as day. Humans still resolve things with fighting and war and it is the probability at this point, wouldn't you say?

So, your choice is to react in fear or to be aware of what is happening and to make your own choices. There have and will be times ahead when the world will seem like it is collapsing around you and everyone is living in fear.

At that point realize what is happening.

Peripatetic Existence

Don't be attached to how you think your life should be.

Be like the vagabond who is open to new things.

Control is an Illusion

Controlling anything is not possible.

Stop trying to.

Trying to control existence is like telling the ocean what to do.

It doesn't work.

Possibility

Engage your imagination

by believing that the impossible

is possible.

You are the energy of possibility.

You are the energy of choice.

Give it All Up

Do you want to explore the nature of reality and existence?

~Then give up what you think it's all about~

Do you wish to connect with what is sacred?

~Then give up your holy texts~

Do you want to know what love truly is?

~Then give up your definitions of love~

Do you wish to connect with your essence?

~Then let go of who and what you think you are~

And so it begins.

No one ever said this journey was going to be easy but it's the best ride around.

And it's infinitely worth it.

The Energy of Choice

The energy of choice is this:

That when a choice is made there will be manifestation.

It may not happen immediately but it will. There is that clarity and movement into definition.

Think of it this way:

A man walks into a pub and orders a pint. The beer is poured and set on the counter for the man. Observe the space in time between when the man chose to go to the pub and the time the beer is in his grasp. There is the process of creation.

But just because the beer did not manifest immediately when the thought arose does not mean that the physical manifestation was not coming.

Observe how the man chose to put himself in a place or environment where his choice would manifest. Notice he did not walk into a video store. He walked into a pub. Notice he did not pour the pint himself or brew the beer or grow the hops or direct the bartender on how to pour the beer. The man did not talk about his choice or go through a process of "should I…" or "shouldn't I…." There was no need to. No need to control things.

He made his choice, part of which was to be part of the movement or allowing the movement of the universe to bring to him what he wanted. And it was allowed. If he did not accept and allow the beer into his life it would not be there.

This applies to things big and small in our lives.

What choices are you making?

What choices are you endlessly justifying?

What would it mean to simply choose and forgo the whole process of justification (and how much energy would that free up?)

Giving to Yourself What You Need

One of the main things I've learned in my life so far is something that most people won't find impressive or sexy.

It's not something that's going to appeal to a many either.

But it is something essential to any progress you will make on your journey to realizing a deeper understanding of yourself and existence.

And it's something I've mentioned before which is simply this:

You cannot get from anyone else what you must give to yourself.

Examine your life and choices and observe where your fears are. Observe where you have perspectives of lack or insufficiency.

Observe the blocks in your physical, emotional, mental and spiritual self that need healing. Examine your self-worth and just how accepting and loving you are of yourself.

Observe where you are "needy" or repeating a pattern that is no longer serving any purpose for you. Observe any areas where you are stagnating.

And then choose to go in a new direction and let your choices and life reflect that.

I recall a time in my life I was left utterly devastated. My first adult relationship was a very intense experience, an overseas soulmate connection that ended for different reasons but we were a mirror for internal things that needed healing. And when it ended, I was an emotional wreck and tried to fill that void by looking for "the One" everywhere I went.

But the positive from the relationship was that is showed me exactly what I needed to work on in myself: *I was emotionally needy*. And that was not a place I wanted to be as it would only attract more of the same and it was not a satisfying way to live. So eventually I acknowledged that and chose to heal myself.

Being honest with yourself creates clarity and at that point there is movement to being whole and healed. Clarity is a reflection of health.

Your journey in life is an opportunity to become aware of yourself. To become truly aware of yourself and be conscious of your choices.

And from that perspective what is sexier than that?

Do not forget to include this in the story of your life:

"...And then something magical happened..."

And be open for it.

Allow it.

Belief Systems

It's interesting how powerful belief systems are.

The Ganges River is one the most polluted water sources in the world. Human cremation occurs at Varanasi and carries downstream. It contains large scale industrial waste, farm pesticides and sewage throughout it.

And yet millions use it a source to sustain their life and for them it is holy. They pray in it. Bathe and clean in it. Play in it. Even drink from it.

And there are fatalities certainly, but if people from the West were to use it that way the death toll would be far higher.

Advanced Concepts in Healing

It is the mind that needs healing, not your body.

Recognize the body has an innate and inherent ability to be in balance and restore itself to balance if allowed. It is the mind that interferes and creates imbalance in your life. And that can easily manifest as illness, physical or otherwise.

When people want to heal from cancer they should obviously eat organic, nutritious foods, go raw more, take larger doses of vitamin C and drink lots of clean spring water. They should do things that help to heal like bring oxygen into the body and laugh more. That goes without saying.

When people get sick it is an opportunity to connect deeper with themselves and explore new, more empowering ways of living.

But recognize it is not the body so much as the mind that needs addressing.

Use the mind to direct the essence of energy that you are to healing your physical, emotional and mental states. To make shifts into health and ease and a "yes" acceptance of life.

Consciously apply your mind to bring the energy that you are into your life and create shifts. Give it that direction and choose it. Choose health and choose You and when your choices reflect that and you are that energy, your body will be in balance.

Allow the energy that you are to express itself in the world. It just feels good.

And doing this opens the door to living a very long and happy life, much longer than people are currently living. It opens the door to new ways of living.

No one really does this but you can be among the first. And it's not simply about healing but about creating the life you truly want.

Imagine

what would happen

if you just let your life happen.

The Energy Behind Perception

Everything you see with the physical perception of your sight is being held together or created with an energy that you are not separate from.

That includes the sidewalk and park and building you see. It includes the people you see and all activity and movement. It includes your body and relationships. And all of your other perceptions and movements.

And how much energy do you think you are expending to uphold the perspective that you are separate from everything else?

The current perspective of humanity is of a contracted and very limited perspective of existence. It does afford us some interesting experiences but it is also one we will grow out of when we are done experiencing it and choose something more.

Explore the relationship between emptiness, form and perception if it interests you. It leads to so much.

Querencia

There is an interesting Spanish word that I love. It is Querencia.

Querencia has been described as a place where one feels secure and where our strength is drawn from. It is a place of ease in which we know exactly who we are, and the place from which we speak our deepest truth.

In bullfighting parlance, it describes when a bull stops reacting out of fear to the Matador but pauses to center himself. From here it becomes almost impossible to kill the bull and a dangerous time for the Matador.

It is interesting that as a verb "querer" means "to desire." And it is infinitely worth pausing and asking the basic question of what that deeper part of ourself wants.

Desire in this context is not the petty desire of trying to fulfill your craving for Doritos or playing a game of your ego-personality but something much more.

It speaks to the very heart and essence of life. The movement of your soul.

What do you desire to create, to feel, to express and be in the world? What is possible for your desire to open you up to?

Querencia is a state of being. It is your place of power. It is that place you can choose to live from.

It is that movement and evolution of you as you.

Live Forever if You Want

A moment of pause.

A moment of seeing the larger perspective.

A moment of stillness. Of beingness.

Beyond "just chillin'".

A moment that dissolves the world and all your troubles away.

Connecting with who you are.

Cultivating that as a lifestyle. Embracing that simplicity.

You can live forever if you want to.

Life is just a moment of time.

Everything is here this moment.

Realize that at some point time ceases to exist.

That Which Cannot Be Measured

Swim in the ocean.

The waters stretch to the horizon.

You are part of something so big

that it cannot be measured.

That is a just a nice thought.

Until you choose to realize it

and it becomes a part of your daily existence.

The awareness of who you are.

The Love that is

"I looked at my life, and it was also a river." -Hermann Hesse

We are all in the habit of trying too hard in our lives. Some more than others.

Breathe deep and see your life for what it is.

Breathe deep and feel where your body carries tensions new, old and ancient.

Breathe deep and see your choices and the manifestation and flow of life.

Have you ever tried to have a fight with the ocean or wind? It doesn't last too long, does it? So, don't bother trying so hard. Stop fighting and resisting and denying whatever you are.

Even in the last 5 seconds of your life you will be choosing and experiencing what you will. And the journey never really ends, does it?

Love is the allowance of all that is. That is the energy of what we are, ultimately. It is for you to observe and know that.

And to choose it.

Poverty Consciousness

There are governments and organizations and people in the world, very well-meaning to be sure, with an intent at 'eliminating poverty'.

What they do not understand is that poverty is not a circumstance but a state of mind or consciousness. A holding pattern of lack.

And no amount of money or intervention will change that. Poverty will remain until humanity shifts its thinking and how it sees itself, as individuals and as a group.

It should be instilled into every child in the family home and in our schools and everywhere – an approach and teaching that is simply this:

CHANGE COMES FROM WITHIN

Without a true understanding of what this means and what allows change there will be a continuance of the problems that plague humanity. Everything from crime to poverty to illness of every kind.

And on the flipside, it is interesting that many people think they have a wealth consciousness but do they really?

Life Observation

Every time I have ever tried to control my existence

it has hurt me.

So, I let go of how I think things should go.

And relax and breathe and open

to more possibilities and choices.

I let go

so that I can allow more.

Passport Stamps

You can travel the world until your passport is unreadable with stamps.

You can build the tallest skyscraper.

You can amass the greatest fortune.

You can be a great parent.

You can live a thousand years or a million lifetimes.

You can live and create in any way you so desire and choose.

That will always be your freedom.

But if you haven't explored and chosen your vulnerability,

if you haven't opened yourself to existence,

if you haven't gone inside yourself and done your homework,

then what have you achieved?

Would You Believe...?

Let me tell you about love.

It is not about the walls you have built to keep you safe and protected.

It is not about the distance you have created between yourself and existence.

Sure, we are here experiencing life. We have learned, laughed, loved, cried, grown. Survived the curveballs life has thrown our way.

But love isn't about holding back or playing it small.

Or waiting till next time.

It isn't about being weak or meek or afraid.

It isn't about repetition and routine. The vacuuming on Tuesday, laundry on Sunday.

It isn't about judging yourself for that pimple on your forehead or that choice you made that you still regret.

Love isn't about giving your power away to anything 'outside' yourself, the illusion that is this world. The illusion that is your life, your roles, your false identity.

What if I were to tell you that *you are love*. Would you believe it?

What if I were to tell you that what you have always been looking for is simply... you.

Why are you so afraid of your vulnerability?

You can stay in your comfort zone, your shell. You can even play the game of 'this is me expanding my comfort zone'.

Or there is another choice. And it is a choice.

Open yourself to existence.

Choose to go inside yourself.

Connect with the essence you are.

(The simplicity, ease and joy of that.)

Allowance

The state of your true beingness is one of ease.

It goes beyond relaxation. It goes beyond concepts of energy. Beyond perceptions of time and space and cause and effect. Beyond perspectives of limits and limitation.

It is a place of awareness.

And it is already what you are.

Do you doubt this?

Do you not believe that with not even so much as a thought 'allowed' that you could be in another city within the space of a moment?

The Biggest Game in Town

Vegas can't touch it. Neither can Macau.

It's the biggest game in town and everyone is playing it.

Everyone goes through their lives denying their self.
Denying their essence.

And it's one big game isn't it? Even in the spiritual and religious circles the game is in full effect, giving lip service to what love is.

And the stakes are large. They could not be more. And the thing is just by playing the game you will lose every time.

And everyone who plays this game are too busy with everything to even realize they are playing it. This is the current state of humanity.

When someone moves to a point where they want to explore beyond the distractions and contractions of life, beyond giving the mind more candy and the turning away from themself where can they go?

Where can you find yourself?

Is it under a rock? Or at the corner store?

Is it in a book or movie or self-help guru?

Is it in a relationship? In sex?

In your friends or family or neighbours?

Your job or career or hobby?

Is it skydiving or taking up MMA?

Is it in a war-ravaged country?

Is it flirting with death by smoking, drinking, popping Percocet, and the million other ways humans choose to reduce themselves and die?

Is it in some obscure reference in some ancient text yet to be uncovered?

Is it in some religious teaching? What do you think?

Yes, the world is your reflection but you will not find yourself in any of these places.

The only place to find yourself is in the deepest and scariest place of all.

Within.

Find Something That is True for You

Do you think your circumstances define you?

Maybe to the point they are reflective of your choices and give you an environment from which to create.

But circumstance is fleeting and does not mean much.

Whether you are rolling in the lap of luxury on a yacht off the Italian coast or dying of liver cancer as a homeless person in the streets of Acapulco, ultimately it matters not.

Granted these are two very different life experiences. But do you think it is impossible for that man in Acapulco to laugh at life and be happy, to refuse to give his power away and be the author of his own life?

Do you think it is impossible for a businesswoman on that yacht to be bored and unfulfilled with life and her billions and wish to give it all up for something -anything- new?

What really matters to you?

Is it money? It can be nice but it comes as a result of who you are and your choices. It is not a reason for living or waking up in the morning.

Is it upholding a role you are trying to convince others or yourself that you are? That steals your energy and time and is a losing game.

Ask yourself – what truly matters to you?

Are you tired of living the same way and not really satisfied? Well, you are free to go in another direction. Aren't you?

Go deep and keep asking yourself until you find something that you feel is true for you.

That man in Acapulco would be one of the most expansive individuals who ever lived if even for a moment he achieved a moment of clarity and ease where he was able to connect with himself and laugh not just at all the terrible shit in his life but the joy of being alive, seeing beyond the surface.

What is important to you? What do you want out of this big grand thing called life? Why are you here?

Remember, this life you are living.... one day you will not be.

You do not need to measure your life and choices or judge things. But you do need to look at yourself in the mirror and ask something you have been avoiding for a long time. Don't you?

It was an ancient Greek temple inscription: Know thyself.

Isn't it time to find out who you truly are?

Anything is Possible

"You are here and warm
But I could look away and you'd be gone
Cause we live in a time
When meaning falls in splinters from our lives
And that's why I've traveled far
'Cause I come so together where you are"
> – the song "Sentimental Lady" by Bob Welch

Even as a boy I had a certain feeling about time. A distinct sense that life is but a moment in time. And over the decades this particular perception hasn't diminished but grown.

You could even say all of time is a but a moment.

This moment called now.

How could that possibly be?

Past and future are but judgments made from the now. A perception. A choice. It also speaks to the oneness of existence.

And you wish to time travel and be in the year 1890? Or 2068? That's as easy as being in this year, is it not? So, what keeps us firmly rooted to this particular time?

Simply this: the mind.

Anything is possible if you but suspend the mind... for a moment.

Do You Choose to Limit Love?

Love is not what you think it is.

It is not loving only those who love you back.

It is not loving what is "good" only.

It is not really an emotion.

It is not about allowing your fear to take over your life and reacting to events.

And it is not about controlling the circumstances of your life and choices.

If you try to define love then it escapes you.

Love simply is (all and everything.)

The allowance of every possibility and choice.

A man walks into a nightclub in Orlando and murders 49 people and injures many others while revelling in social media response.

And it is hard not to react. It is hard not to get angry and be fearful. But isn't anger and fear part of the whole problem? Doesn't it perpetuate a vicious cycle of hate and destruction and imbalance?

The world will always have this type of violence until we heal ourselves. Individually and collectively.

And it begins with you, this moment.

Do you choose to limit love?

Or are you willing and able to see beyond the violence into the heart of things? Are you willing to see beyond the perception of separation and differences into what brings us all together?

We do not have to agree with the choice of a Hitler or a Manson or a Mateen or anyone else. Their choice is their choice. Not yours. Tragedies like this are great opportunities to realize our own choices and to find our own clarity.

But if you choose not to love (everyone) then isn't it just a game of selection? Isn't it just a distortion of what love is and what you are capable of?

(and do you not think that somewhere in your many lifetimes incarnated here on this planet, past and future, that you are not a thief, rapist or murderer yourself?)

What do you choose to express to the world and experience?

Fear?   There is enough of that in the world. Almost everyone chooses that and allows the choices of others to become their own choices.

Or do you choose love?

Love is limitless. And it is a limitless way to live. Without barriers or boundaries.

And it begins with you.

Dreaming and Desire

"I had some dreams, they were clouds in my coffee, clouds in my coffee, and... (chorus)"

-Carly Simon, "You're So Vain"

Life is but a dream.

There is more truth in the children's song "Row, row, row your boat" than one might imagine.

And you may achieve your dreams or not; you may create new dreams or abandon your dreams altogether; you may make your life the dream, or not.

There is always the possibility to reinvent yourself anew or go in a new direction.

The thing is this: Your life is the dream. And if you are not allowing the movement of your desire and energy into your life then you are cutting yourself off from something essential.

And at that point you may as well kiss your life good-bye as it is all but over.

Energy, Health and Creation

To move beyond technique and the endless trying in your life means to simply allow.

To simply do it.

It is not a thought or process, although you can do it that way.

But that is a complication. A mental process, not real creation.

Go into the simplicity and simply choose.

Everything else is just a game.

A game of disempowerment that humanity has become addicted to like heroin.

Simply do it. Make the choice. There is nothing to figure out.

Between now and tomorrow your reality can change completely.

But what are you willing to allow into your life?

Do you not believe that the energy of the universe that creates the stars and planets and sustains all life will not support you in your choices?

Get in touch with this energy, for you on not separate from it.

It is your perception of separation that fuels and keeps you in your limitations.

The Relaxation Response

Relaxation is a choice.

Cultivated as a practice it can be a response

 to the stimulus of a world that can easily pull us

from our place of being.

Relaxation can be an opening into awareness.

An opening into simplicity.

An opening into more.

If you choose it and go in that direction.

Exploring Yourself as Energy

Everything in your life is viewed from the perspective of your physicality.

Think about it for a minute.

Our bodies.   Our interactions with others and our environment.

The necessity for food, water, air, shelter, clothing.

Sickness, health, well-being.

Philosophy and religion.

Movement. Cause and effect.

Time, space.

But what happens when we open to a different perspective, a new perspective, one of energy? What begins to happen to our relationship with all of these things?

When you choose – and the word *choose* is key here – when you choose to see yourself as energy, as awareness, then everything opens up.

Everything.

Call it what you want.

A Radical Honesty

Going deeper is not about reading books, going on retreats in the Costa Rican rainforest, quoting the Bhagavad Gita, ACIM or Bible or wearing the sexiest mala or man-bun.

Going deeper is not about OHM-ing or getting caught up in a role or distractions.

It is also not about giving your power away to people like John of God and John de Ruiter or being a "follower" of Oprah or thinking that Deepak Chopra, Dr. Oz or the Dalai Lama have answers that you do not.

Going deeper is about being honest with yourself. Being real.

Call it a radical honesty.

Is it time you start walking a new path in your life?

Consciousness

Consciousness is the awareness of existence.

It is the knowing that you are much, much more than what you have been defined or limited by. It is the realization that you exist beyond the physical, mental, emotional and spiritually manifested aspects of your existence, beyond any one particular defined circumstance or reality.

When someone observes their life without judgment it becomes clear how their choices create the reality in which they exist. They become aware of the interconnection of their energy with all that exists and the choice is made to move with that energy, that movement and understanding. There is no longer a necessity or desire to see themselves as separate from anything since energy, no matter how you define it, is all that is.

Realize that the reality in which you live is a reflection of your awareness. If you want to change it, simply do so. Every perspective or perception is a limitation of your awareness or level of consciousness. That includes the limits you have chosen to exist by such as death.

Death defines so much about how we see ourselves and it seems to be the grand, inevitable and terminal conclusion to our lives on this planet. And such a serious and somber finality at that. The idea of death is only a perspective or belief that can be moved beyond. It is an illusion like all other perceptions. You do not have to wait until your physical body ceases to be to explore what is beyond death.

The realization that you are energy is this exploration, the movement beyond limitations. It is inevitable you will remember who you truly are, but why not do it in this lifetime?

The idea of interconnection and oneness remains that — an idea for yourselves — until your energy is extended into creating that reality through your choices. Some people in the spiritual circles have an intellectual grasp of the essence of existence, the oneness energy, call it what you will. But how many empower themselves to consciously choose it all the time and live from this state?

Love energy is an energy of inclusion and allowance of all that is and the choice will inevitably be made to move beyond how you see yourself and to see what your relationship is with everything, including God-Goddess-All That Is. It is mainly a question of when.

Observation without judgment will expand your lives and lead you to an appreciation of yourselves and the realization of your true nature. The brilliance you are.

Creation and Time

A Neolithic era hunter has an idea for a new type of weapon design. Through a series of attempts she finally creates it and her tribe benefits from it and the design is carried on for future generations.

Different teachers from ancient Mediterranean lands allow their existence to be a light and example for others by offering a new way of seeing and being in the world. Not just in their own time but for thousands of years after.

A seamstress in medieval France creates a variance in design that leads to a new fashion trend that defines an era and influences fashion, design, and living to the present time.

A man lives a safe, monotonous life and works for the same insurance company for 40 years. He has the average 2.2 kids and 2.9 TVs and dies peacefully in his sleep at age 78.

Through their existence these people brought forth something into their existence, ushered the energy forth and manifested it. They created it.

It is the year 2015 and I am sitting here watching an episode on a TV made in Thailand. The show is Miami Vice which originally aired in 1984 with actors who were born in the 40s and 50s. I am wearing a t-shirt and pants that were designed and then created by someone in another country a few years ago, drinking black tea that was harvested by farmers in Sri Lanka, packed in the UK, imported into Mississauga, Ontario and then shipped to an Edmonton warehouse and transported to a local store. An employee at the store put the box of tea on the shelf and a cashier swiped the box when I paid for it.

All of this is only part of a chain of hundreds and thousands of people doing jobs, living their lives, manifesting themselves in the way they are. And this interconnection is with everything, everywhere, all the time.

What is your movement and expression through time?
Do you really think for a 'second' that you are not a part of everything around you or that your choices do not ripple out into the world?

In whatever way you manifest yourself as, your life has meaning and is integral to all that is. All of our creations go through this process we call time. We apply ourselves through the movement called time, we infuse all of existence with our choices.

Until a point is reached when the perception of time no longer exists in the way it has, or at all. For time is a creation and oneness is a choice.

Open yourself to all that is and play with energy and perception and your understanding of things. Extend a thought or idea into your reality and see where it leads. Or plant a thought or idea into your consciousness and see how it grows.

Extend yourself back or forward in time and see what happens. Extend your energy to a grandparent when they were your age and needed a hug, or to your future self during a challenging time, or to anywhere or anyone.

Extend your energy.

Technology vs. Consciousness

As humans we love our technology. It adds convenience and excitement to our lives. And we are adopting it as fast as it comes out for the most part.

Soon seemingly everything in our lives will be connected with technology. The Internet of Things (IoT) is a term being used to describe part of it. And it is exciting to watch as it unfolds.

Having said that it is worth mentioning that this development and advancement of technology that humanity is choosing is not the only way we can evolve, grow and explore. Where do you think the inter-dimensional factors of the universe come from? They come from us. What is within us.

An example is teleportation. Eventually there will be technology that will allow people to travel to other points of time-space on the planet and other places. It will not be for a long while but it is coming if we survive as a species.

Or there is the other way to teleport. Through a shift in consciousness. Without the use of technology. In terms of communication, telepathy and our sense of knowing are (unused) abilities we have foregone, choosing instead cell phones, texting, etc.

Like everything it will come down to what we choose. Collectively and individually. It is not an 'either-or' scenario and I am not saying do not use technology. Embrace it in whatever way you will but choose how you will use it in your daily life and be aware of your choices.

Do not use it as a way to disempower yourself. Do not give your power away to technology or think it is the only way. Remember it is only a tool.

Technology of any kind has its limits and will only take us so far. The alternative is to explore what is within.

The Relationship of Things

We live in a very 'causal' way. Not casual but causal. Cause and effect.

Everything is relative to something else.

We have a defined and perceived relationship with everyone and everything. All of our mental and emotional activity and perceptions are in terms of relationship with another, with something else.

Think about it:

When you walk down a street and someone unknown walks by they are viewed as a stranger. Someone unknown.

'Movement' and 'growth' in your life is seen in relation to perceptions of the past/future or physical objects.

'Money' is seen as something outside of yourself and something to accumulate.

'Patience' implies an enduring some hardship or trial with another person or situation.

'Anger' is in relation to some other person or circumstance. A reaction.

'Health' is seen as the absence of disease.

The 'environment' you are in is seen as external to yourselves. Not part of your energy.

And we define ourselves by our judgments, our many relationships. Our separation.

Ultimately this 'relationship' is not with another person or something outside but with ourselves.

When the choice is made to start seeing things as energy and you observe the inter-relationship of existence, then there is movement into new ways of living and being in the world. New ways of seeing. There is no longer the necessity to hold to rigid patterns or behavior or to make judgments about everything.

The experience and exploration of life becomes an exploration of our relationship with everything. An appreciation of the oneness.

And what is more exciting than that?

Parable: The Traveler

There was once a young man who one day chose to set out upon a great journey to travel the world. He wanted to see what this world had to offer and see all the sights and meet amazing people and experience life to the fullest.

His journey took him far and wide: across great plains, wilderness, mountains, deserts, across seas and oceans and he visited many villages and explored cities he had not known existed.

He was a little restless in nature and did not stay in one place too long but was open to meeting new people and making friends and appreciated what came his way in life.   It was not always easy but he made a living mainly as a trader and shared with the people he met stories of his travels and thoughts and life.

Over the years he visited and explored many countries and lands, many things of the world: the tastes and flavors and sights and scents and experienced life in his way.   He had explored the world and come to know it. He had grown in understanding and awareness and had no regrets but as he began to feel older he reminisced how his life path was a choice to live in the way he had.

He had not chosen a family or to stay in one place and nurture friendships or community.   Not that there was anything wrong with his choice, he felt. But he began to feel alone in the world.

One day he embarked on a journey to a distant land he had heard reports and hints of for many years but was not sure it was real or fictitious. Perhaps this land he had heard of was just the remnant of myth and legend.   A story or invention of the human desire to go beyond the usual.

He had been walking alone for days and weeks into new terrain. To a place where others feared and did not travel. What was to come he did not know but something within him wanted to find it.

The sun was shining. He looked back at his footsteps in the sand and reflected on his movements in this lifetime... he remembered the faces and friends and lovers and people he had come to know in his life.   He remembered the places and experiences and the flow of his life but he asked himself if he had truly accomplished what he had set out to do?

Looking forward there was nothing but expanse of land, the horizon stretched out to forever.   Perhaps the journey would go on forever he thought. And with that thought he took a step and carried on his journey to this unknown place. And as he did so the realization came over him that all of the places and people he had known in his life.... they were part of him as he was part of them and all.

This was the place he had been journeying to all of his life. It was not a land or place in time but an awareness.

He paused, lifted his head to the sun and smiled.

Parable: The Inmate and the Guard

In the remote hills of a country there was once a small but well-fortified prison where prisoners were sometimes sent.

One of the prisoners was a man the guards respected.   He was a mystery to them.   They were told to keep guard over him and they did.

Over the years the inmate and a particular guard grew to know each other, not in the way close friends do but certainly in familiarity as they often played backgammon together. They liked each other and spend most of their time together was in silence.

One day the inmate asked the guard a question, "Who is more free? Me or you?"

The guard looked up from the board and attempted to scrutinize his unflinching gaze.

"Well I am not the one sleeping behind iron bars every night, am I?"

"Well I can assure you, these feeble bars do not impede my existence much. At night I dream and explore how I choose. And in the day, I choose my state of mind and I am free. Like a bird soaring.   I do not see myself as a victim of circumstance. But you are charged with the responsibility and duty of making sure I do not escape. One day these bars will cease to be part of my physical reality."

The guard laughs impetuously but there is a touch of fear in his sound. The inmate knows the seed is planted. What he has said will grow into something as the guard contemplates it. And sure enough, over time it does.

The years pass. And it could have happened in many ways but the inmate's words come true. The country's government changes power and he is let go. The prison ceased to be part of his experience.

Parable: The Freediver

There is a freediver who lives along the coast of her country and enjoys a life of sun and simplicity. The things of this world she embraces but never allows them to be distractions from her natural and relaxed way of being and her passion for freediving.

Every morning she practices what is for her an art, a meditation, a love affair with the ocean, a connection to the greater self.   Years ago she was active in competition around the world but gave it up as over time it became her personal practice and way of living and being. Exploring the depth and mystery of the ocean, her relationship with the ocean and awareness of herself.

She plunges down into the water with one breath and goes deep.   Deeper than she ever has. A breath of air that supports her until she resurfaces minutes later. Sometimes a friend watches on the shore but most often she is alone. She is aware and knows that the exploration goes far beyond diving into the depths... her journey is one of self-realization, deepening her awareness and understanding herself and existence.

And this is not so much a story but as her life progresses, she opens to a true understanding of herself and her life becomes an expression of love and the essence she is. And all who come to know her feel her love and joy of life and are better for it.

Excerpt from audio:

The Limitless Self: Create the Life of Your Dreams

The Garden Meditation

"Find a comfortable place and take a few deep breaths, opening your mind, body and awareness.   With the simplicity of a choice bring ease into this moment of time and feel it permeate every part of you…. Let go of anything that contracts any part of your existence and feel your energy and perception broaden and deepen….

Feel the heat of the sun on your skin and the air fill your lungs as you breathe deeper and soften your energy. Take a moment to connect with your energy. Feel how there is no clear end to your energy, it just extends out to envelop everything around you and more.

You are in a garden with lush vegetation and green.   It is a place you feel instantly connected with as you notice the vibrancy of the place. Butterflies and dragonflies float by…. birds sing their songs cheerfully and there is a spring of gently flowing fresh water nearby…. a mix of different flower scents in the air…. the trees sway gently with the wind and there is an abundance of healthy fruits and vegetables and nuts.   Enough to easily support the life of many.

You walk through the garden and your feet enter the soil.   It feels nourishing.   Sustaining. You feel whole and complete here and your energy is at one with the Garden.   You want to live here and nurture the garden and watch it grow and bask in it all for you realize that *the Garden is you*.

You smile as you lift your gaze to the sun and take it all in. Your energy flows.   Love grows…. You feel yourself as an energy that can grow in any way.   Limitlessness. Energy flowing through time and beyond.

Your nostrils enjoy the smell of the soil…. so earthy and rich, almost a magical, sparkling quality.   You know that whatever is planted here will grow and sustain life. Everything here is fertile and the fruit is ripe.   You take a bite out of a piece of fruit or vegetable and enjoy its delicious taste; you feel it enter and nourish the cells of your body and your cells vibrate with thanks and wellness. You walk over to the spring and take a drink of cool water. It not only quenches your thirst but invigorates your body, increases your vitality and you feel great joy in being here and being alive.

This is the Garden of Life and you feel yourself open up…. You know that your life will grow in whatever direction you choose and you will grow beyond anything you can imagine.

Allow your life to blossom and expand. The Garden is you and you are the Garden.

And as you breathe in deeply and exhale, return to your surroundings and carry with you this knowledge and awareness.   And make your life your greatest dream."

About the Author

I was born in 1976 and as a boy grew up on the Saskatchewan prairies. It's a place that's often not appreciated and even ridiculed for being flat or that place people drive through on their way to somewhere else. The roads do stretch out in long lines and the landscape is not as varied as some places, but it has a beauty and majesty all its own: endless golden wheat fields shimmer and ebb to the horizon; in places there are easy, rolling hills shouldering the roads and the sky seems to open up right from the very ground. It's fiercely rugged with the extreme seasons and a quiet serenity and expansiveness that opens up something deep within, if you let it.

The countryside and smaller city setting are places where you can meet yourself. For me it was home. And it is from here I observed my life and existence and started to wake up.

My life has been a journey of remembrance and awakening.

As a boy I wondered about the limits of what is possible and would simply observe the world or sit in meditation before a flame and try to move things with my mind. As a teenager I fell in love with books like the **Tao Te Ching**. After high school I was drifting through life, unsatisfied, frustrated and unhappy and it wasn't until I healed myself of a critical illness in my 20s that I started making the choice to remember again.

Starting in 2006 I explored various spiritual teachings and knowledge full-time for several years, as a way to reconnect with the deeper aspects of myself. One of my passions is energy healing and work.

My website www.theradiantself.wordpress.com has been active since 2014 and this is my fourth book (but first non-fiction). The previous one was called **Ayama's Journey: The Nature of Reality** (2016) and deals with spirituality, awareness and growth.